NO MORE ACCEPTANCE

Uncovering and Overcoming the Pattern of the World

Bradley Stubbs

Bradley Stubbs

NO MORE ACCEPTANCE

Uncovering and Overcoming the Pattern of the World

Bradley Stubbs

Christian Publishing House

Cambridge, Ohio

Unless otherwise stated, Scripture quotations are from ESV: Study Bible: English standard version. Wheaton, Ill: Crossway Bibles; NIV Study Bible. Zondervan Pub. House, 2011; NKJV Study Bible. (2018). Nashville, TN: Thomas Nelson.

NO MORE ACCEPTANCE: Uncovering and Overcoming the Pattern of the World by Bradley Stubbs

ISBN-13: **9798589400595**

Table of Contents

Acknowledgments

I want to thank my beautiful and amazing wife Gracie for being so supportive and encouraging throughout our lives together in ministry and for always pushing me to fulfill the call God has laid upon my heart. I want to thank my family and friends for always being there when I needed someone to talk to and for giving me honest feedback to help me grow. My parents and my dear friend Taylor Moeller have especially guided me through some really difficult seasons in my life and helped me become the person I am today. I want to thank my church family for pushing and challenging me to live out God's call on my life to the fullest extent and for being so loving and caring to Gracie and myself throughout everything life throws at us. Most importantly, I want to thank my LORD and Savior Jesus Christ for saving me from my sins when I absolutely did not deserve it and for giving me the gifts, wisdom, and strength to share what He has laid upon my heart for others. Thank you to everyone who takes the time to read this book, and I earnestly pray God speaks to you as He has spoken to me. To God be the glory forever and ever, Amen.

Introduction: No More Acceptance

As I have grown in my Christian faith, a couple of verses always keep coming back to me. I have pondered on these verses for years and have really sought to discover what they mean for myself and for others in the world today. Those verses are Romans 12:1-2, which state, "Therefore, I urge you, brothers and sisters, in view of God's mercy, to offer your bodies as a living sacrifice, holy and pleasing to God—this is your true and proper worship. Do not conform to the pattern of this world but be transformed by the renewing of your mind. Then you will be able to test and approve what God's will is—his good, pleasing and perfect will." (NIV) A few things have really stuck with me in this verse: what is a living sacrifice? What pattern does the world have?, and how do I renew my mind?

Many of you may have the same questions, or if you just read those verses for the first time, I am sure you are thinking the same thing. As I have prayed and sought God's will in writing this book, I hope to shed light on each of these questions and give us tools on how to not conform to the world we live in today but to stand firm in God's Word, living out His truth in all we do. The first big question I want to try and tackle, which is also my heart in writing this book, is what pattern does the world live in? We have to answer this question before we can figure out the other two and, more importantly, for us to figure out how to live the way God is calling us to.

First, the world simply means the way people live and act without Jesus in their life. The world we live in is inherently evil since the Fall of man and if we choose to not live by God's Word, then we will live according to the evil of the world. I have concluded that the pattern of this world can be summed up like this: the world will always seek to accept sin as right and those that oppose it as wrong. We look at the Bible, and time and time again, when the Israelites took their eyes off God and decided to live how they wanted to, they slowly started accepting the sin that was in the world around them. They began worshipping idols, having sexually immoral relationships, and participating in pagan practices. All these sinful acts were common in the world they lived in, and those that practiced these things were accepted by the world, and those that did not were rejected.

So, the Israelites gave in to the pattern of the world and started accepting the sinful lifestyles as well. When they did this, and when we do this today, acceptance of sin leads into promotion of sin. It was not long until the Israelites not only participated in these sinful acts, but they started to promote them as the way their people should live. This is what Romans 12 speaks to us when God's Word warns us not to conform to the pattern of this world. When we start accepting sin, it will not be long until we start promoting it as the way we are supposed to live. There are many reasons that we fall into this pattern of the world, and I think the main one in our world today is that the world has convinced us that to truly love someone else or yourself is to accept whatever lifestyle you or they desire to live in and never try to convince them or yourself to live differently. The world will tell you that to do that would be offensive to that person, or you may be trying to change who you or they truly are. This is the lie of the world that acceptance = love and that I hope to uncover throughout this book.

There seems to be a common belief in our world today that if we are to show love to people then we are to fully accept them as they are. This belief is not wrong as each of us is sinners, yet Jesus loves us anyway and died on the cross for all of us. We are called to reach out to and show love to people despite what they have done, where they were raised, and what kind of personality they have. Where the world has warped this belief is when someone goes so far as to say, "to love someone means we should accept any lifestyle they are living and tell them to live any differently would be offensive, thus not loving that person." Think about all the movies and TV shows that have come out recently. Many of them have foul language, have one or more main characters that are either living a homosexual lifestyle or debating it, have sexually immoral relationships, and portray the "party life" as the one we should all be running after.

The music we listen to today is commonly filled with foul language, wording that implies drug use is the cool way to live, language that is downgrading to women, and sends messages that violence is actually the answer in many cases. Billboards and advertisements are filled with images and messages portraying women as sexual objects. Not to mention, our friends and family that have been nailed with the hammer of acceptance from the world also feel they should drag us into accepting what society does so they can feel like they are not the only ones conforming. This gives them some peace about their choice knowing more people are also accepting what the world is portraying as correct.

We fill ourselves with this information all throughout the day many times without even thinking about it. What happens is that over time, our minds have heard these sinful things so much in a positive light that our minds start questioning if they really are wrong. We start convincing ourselves that these actions are not really that bad, and Jesus loved sinners, so we should just accept people's sinful behaviors and keep living our lives. I mean, Jesus forgives, right? So, who cares if other people or we are not following the Bible exactly as God lays it out? I mean, we should be able to live however we want if it brings us happiness, right? Isn't that what God would want for us, to be happy?

If the last few sentences sound like a similar conversation you had in your head recently, you are not alone. Many of us have this conversation or one like it with ourselves and maybe even our friends recently. This is normal as the world is continually beating us down with the hammer of acceptance. If we do not accept everyone's lifestyle, then that means we are showing hate to that person or that group of people. It means that we think we are better than that person or those people. It means that we are small-minded. I want to encourage each one of you reading this book that if you feel like this hammer of acceptance is coming down on you, and you are a nail just waiting to get hit over and over until you are nailed right into the place where society wants you, the Bible offers us some very helpful insight when it comes to acceptance of sin and how to live as lights in a world of darkness. I want to explore some common ways we fall into this world's pattern, which is acceptance of sin and how to overcome those barriers.

Hope Misplaced

One of the tools the devil will use to get people to accept the pattern of the world is to give people a false sense of hope when they feel hopeless. You ever wonder why political candidates work so hard to try and win over people in poverty, people that have been hurt recently, or those in low places in life? They know that these people feel like they are without hope. They are vulnerable. So, when someone approaches them and offers hope and a better life if they support their cause, why would they not jump all over that? Unfortunately, if all political campaigns were completely truthful and hope could really be offered from political campaigns or government alone, we would not still have millions across the globe in poverty, high crime rates in certain cities, and people living in terrible conditions, feeling there is no hope left for them.

The truth is that real hope can only be found in Jesus and a life dedicated to following Him alone. The world will constantly promote the lie that true hope, joy, and peace will only come when you conform to their ideas and beliefs or the pattern of this world. Time and time again, people will fall victim to this lie because they do not know of the true hope found in Jesus, and the thought of any kind of hope, joy, and peace sounds so appealing to them that they are prepared to support whatever they have to if they can attain these things. This is another reason why Jesus calls us to go and tell of the hope that is in Him to all the nations. People desperately need hope, but they need real, authentic, eternal hope. This is not what the world is going to offer them, and if we as Christians do not go to the nations to tell of the hope we have in Jesus that is freely available to them as well, then the world will surely tell them of the "hope" they can have if they follow the things the world believes to be correct.

When I was younger, I was picked on quite a bit. I wore glasses, had a unibrow, and was super scrawny. I mean, for middle school kids, I was basically golden for all kinds of jokes and put-downs. I got really lonely in middle school, and although I grew up in a loving Christian home and attended church all my life, I started to let the world get the best of me, and I begin to have a sense of hopelessness. I believed that if I could just find a way to be popular, all my problems would be solved. I would have friends and fame, and what more could an almost high schooler want? The world had convinced me that true hope and joy would only come from being popular and being good at what the world loved. Where I grew up, the world loved football.

Every Friday night, the stands were full, and for the days that followed, people in the town talked about the events that took place in the football game. So, what did I do? I worked really hard to make the football team. In my mind, this was my hope of finding happiness and love in this world. Now, being as scrawny as I was, I was not going to play any kind of big tackling position. What I did know how to do, however, was kick. I had played soccer all my life, and I had gotten good at it. So, I trained for hours and hours every chance I could to become the best kicker I could be. By my freshman year, I was not only on the football team, but I was the only freshman that got to dress out for varsity. I felt like I had made it.

My life started to radically change. I begin to have a confidence I had not had before, and I started to have a bunch of new friends. I even had a few girlfriends. I thought life was great, and I had finally found true hope and joy. Fast forward to the summer of my Junior year. I had just had a pretty good season as the starting placekicker, and colleges were interested in signing me to play on their football team. I went to a camp with kickers from all over the nation and rated as a four-star kicker going into my senior year. Life was great, or so I thought. A few weeks before our first game, I was running laps around the field, and I felt my whole body cramp up.

I started to feel really fatigued. I went from making fifty-yard field goals to having trouble making thirty-five-yard field goals. I had no idea what was wrong, and I felt that suddenly all my hopes and dreams were about to come crashing down. I went to the doctor, and they ran several tests, but everything came back negative as if nothing were wrong. This started to make me feel very depressed on top of my already emotionally declining mental state. After weeks of trying to figure out what was wrong, my mom suggested the doctor test my thyroid since that condition ran in my family. It did not take long for the doctor to call back with the shocking news. My thyroid numbers were supposed to be zero to four, and mine were over two hundred! This basically meant that my body was shutting down physically and emotionally as your thyroid controls your hormone function in your body. I asked about the recovery process, and the doctor told me I would have to be on medication for the rest of my life and that it may take months to feel normal again.

I tried not to let this bother me, but I was torn apart on the inside. I personally reflected upon all the things I had filled my life with over the last several years and realized that not a single one of them helped me at this moment. Nothing of this world I filled myself with over the last several years gave me any joy or hope at this moment. The girls I had dated were gone, and the mistakes I made in those relationships would carry with me, my "friends" started to disappear, and I quickly realized that the sport I had invested so much time and effort into was now not so certain. I remember sitting in my room and staring at the ceiling and the realization coming over me that I may lose all the I built my life on over the last few years. Everything I thought brought me joy and hope now just brought me pain and suffering. I thought about Jesus and knew at that moment that without Him in my life, everything else is temporary and pointless. I cried out to Jesus to help me and that I would begin to put my full trust back in Him again. I would live my life with Him guiding me, and whatever His will was, I was prepared to follow it.

The week before our first game, I still felt terrible; it was so bad that I had gained about twenty pounds, and my face was swollen up majorly. I felt like the chipmunk Alvin with the mumps. Needless to say, I was not in tip-top playing condition. The walk-thru before our first game, we practiced field goals. I missed all nine attempts that we took that day. This was the worst I had ever performed. I later learned that the head coach was out recruiting another kicker the day of the game. At our first home game, we had a roaring crowd as usual. I was extremely nervous on the sidelines and really just hoping I would not have to kick any field goals. It was not long into the first half that our offense was struggling, and it was a fourth and long. The coach called on me to kick the field goal. I thought in my head, "coach you really do not want to do that as I am about to embarrass you and myself in front of all these people when I kick this field goal". I remember as I walked out on the field that I prayed that God would help me make this kick. I knew I was weak but that He was strong, and if it were His will, it would happen.

I lined up for the kick, took a deep breath, and waited for the snap. The snap came roaring back. The holder caught the ball and quickly put it into perfect position to receive a kick. I went through my kicking motions and struck the ball. As soon as I hit the ball, I knew I did not get all of it and just stared at the ground. I decided to keep my head up and look and see where it went anyway. To my surprise, it had just enough leg on it, and it was curving toward the middle of the goal posts. In the end, the ball went through the posts. I ended up making eight field goals that year including a career-long forty-one-yarder. I did not have the year I was hoping to have, but I had a blast playing a game I loved with the people I loved. I started to trust God in whatever happened in life, knowing that He was with me with or without football, and that was all that I needed. He was my hope. At the end of the season, I had an offer to play college football at a small school in Illinois. It was basically in the middle of nowhere, and they did not have the most top-notch facilities. What was interesting was that this college was a private Christian school.

After praying about it, I felt led to go to Greenville University and play football, not just because of the football team but because I loved the Christian atmosphere the campus and football team possessed, and I knew I could continue to grow in my faith here without all the distractions of going to a different school. At the end of my three and a half years at Greenville, I had been elected class chaplain all four years, was the vice president of FCA, worked at a local church, and minored in ministry. I found my hope and joy in Jesus Christ, and when I fully trusted him over the things the world offered, I was blessed beyond measure. I was not blessed with lots of money, material things, and I was not at a school with thousands of people that knew me, but I was blessed with a friendship that was true and that I still have to this day, spiritual growth, and a community that loved me. The latter was far better than the first, and if I had to choose all over again, I would choose the same path. True hope will only be found in Jesus Christ and a life dedicated to Him. The world will promise things that looks attractive and seem like they would give us joy, but the world is passing away along with all its desires, but the Word of the LORD is eternal.

"And the world is passing away along with its desires, but whoever does the will of God abides forever." (1 John 2:17, ESV)

Sadly, many of my friends never realized Who true hope comes from. They are still out chasing the things the world tells them will give them hope and joy. After they fail to obtain those things, they often turn to alcohol or substance abuse to ease the pain and emptiness they feel inside, thus falling even deeper into the pattern of sin in the world. This, to their dismay, only widens the void within them. Even the ones that have found great success in what the world promises will give them hope still wake up feeling as if something is missing. If chasing after the things the world promises will give us hope, love and joy really did give us those things, then movie stars, famous singers, and athletes would be the most joyous people on the planet. This is far from the truth, though, as many of these people end up in depression, and several have committed suicide. The world brushes this over as one-off cases or not related to the things they promised would bring fulfillment, but this is exactly the lie I am seeking to uncover. The world has their hope misplaced, and because of this, they neglect the One that can truly give them hope and fall right into the pattern of sin that runs so rampant in our world today.

Another example of hope misplaced from my own life that I feel many of you reading this will be able to relate to and that so often guides people into accepting the pattern of this world is where I placed my hope during my struggle with anxiety and OCD. From a very early age, my parents could tell there was something different about me. Before I left the house, I felt as though I needed to touch the doorknob or the chair eight times and sometimes even twenty-four times. I felt as if I did not do this that something would go wrong that day or that I would lose something valuable in my life. I know how crazy this sounds, and believe me, even while writing this I can laugh to myself about how bizarre this is, but I seriously believed that it would affect me in a negative way if I did not touch certain items an exact number of times. As life went on, this action started bleeding into other areas of my life.

When I was in high school, I felt I had to say certain things to my girlfriend or spend so much time with my her a week or she would leave me when there was no indication on her part that would happen. I believed I had to do so many little rituals each week before my football game, or I would not play well. I tried to ignore this for a while and just try and believe it was normal. The unfortunate thing was my OCD continued to worsen as I entered college. I started to get filled with so much anxiety before I had a game or preached that I would almost be sick. I remember many games tying and untying my cleats sixteen times or more while on the sidelines because I believed if I did not do this, I would miss the kick. Sometimes I was so stuck in my head that I would syce myself out and miss the kick, only furthering the anxiety.

When I realized I have a serious issue was when the intrusive, unwanted thoughts started to come. It was like I could not control my thinking, and my brain was being flooding by thoughts that were completely contrary to my character and who I was. I could be walking to class and then just out of nowhere have this scary, perversive, or morally unacceptable thought fly into my brain. This greatly troubled me, and the more I fought the thoughts off, the stronger they seemed to come. I was so embarrassed and ashamed by these thoughts that I never told anyone what was really troubling me. I felt that as a Christian, I should never experience things like that, and I begin to feel hopeless and alone. I lost sight of Who I should be ultimately looking to for hope, guidance, and strength and instead, turned to the world for a sense of hope.

I spent hours and hours researching all kinds of things that promised to bring joy and peace back into my life. I put all my hope into the things the world promised would heal me. I took several natural substances, loaded up on essential oils, went to therapy, read books, did a workbook, and even started taking prescription medication. All these things, when used properly, can be good and help with anxiety and conditions like OCD, but to my disappointment, I still felt anxious, and I did not have the joy as I had hoped I would or that was promised to me by doing these things. I was, however, blessed to encounter a therapist that was also a Christian. He gave me some of the best advice that still helps me today. He told me that medication and these things I was doing would help with the symptoms of my OCD and anxiety, but it would never completely cure them.

The anxiety would come back in different moments, and these intrusive thoughts would always be there. He told me that I had to have confidence in who God made me to be and who I was in His eyes. See, the world would many times look at the things going on in my head and say there was something wrong with me or that I was a bad person for having these thoughts. The world very likely would tell me that I just need to take this or do that to find the peace and happiness I was looking for. Again, those things may help, but as I found out, they would never give me lasting peace and joy, and that can lead many people to feel even more hopeless. This is especially true if you are like me and you are putting all your hope in these methods or products. He assured me that God looks at the heart. God knows who we really are, no matter what anxiety or intrusive thoughts may flood our brains. If we give our anxiety, worries, fears, and issues to Him with full faith and trust that He will help us through them, we will receive joy and a peace that surpasses all understanding. We could put our hope in the One that would never let us down.

Sure, we will still get attacked with anxiety and intrusive thoughts, but when we do, we have someone who fully understands us, that knows our heart, and is ready to give us His peace to guide us through. When I started putting my hope in God again and having faith that He would help me and that He is with me through it all, I begin to feel a peace and a joy that I never had before, even with taking and doing all the things I was to help with my anxiety.

Many today are still convinced by the lie the world is feeding them that they will find true hope and peace in taking more things or doing new methods. I believe those things work to help with symptoms, but you will never truly be at peace. The more you chase the things the world tells you will cure you and at the same time neglect the only one who is the Great Healer, the farther you will get away from God and the more hopeless you will feel. You will begin to fall into the pattern of the world and start accepting anything the world says will help, which will end up leading you into a much darker place than when you started.

When someone is dealing with anxiety, an internal struggle, or a mental condition, they often look out into the world for hope and guidance but never end up truly finding the joy and peace they were searching for, which leaves them disappointed, beat-down, and more broken.

If we, instead, looked up at the One who provides peace that surpasses all understanding that is not from this world, who completely understands what we are going through, who knows our heart, and put all our faith in Him, we would begin to see a feeling of peace and joy in our lives that we did not know even existed. We can be assured of where we placed our hope.

How Do We Renew Our Minds?

After we examine each method the world uses to get people to accept the pattern of sin, we will look at what we can do to renew our minds in Jesus so we can avoid falling victim to these methods and/or how we can help others avoid falling victim to these methods as well. To renew our minds in Jesus is simply to take in more of Him and at the same time to cleanse ourselves of the things of this world.

One thing about me is that I have always had really bad allergies. During the winter season, it is especially bad. I get lots of sinus congestion, and it makes it hard to breathe and to do normal activities. When I was a teenager and started to have sinus congestion once again, my mom took me to this place to get a detox. I thought it was the strangest thing, especially being a teenage male to go anywhere and get a detox, but I went ahead and went with my mom. After arriving and going to the backroom, they made me put my bare feet into this bucket that was filled with water and apparently lots of natural substances. They instructed me to soak my feet in this water, and after a while I would start to see the water change colors if some of the sinus stuff begin to leave my body.

It did not take long for the water to start turning this nasty green color, and some substances started to show up in the water. Needless to say, I was pretty grossed out but also being a teenage male, pretty fascinated. After the detox was completed, I felt like a new person and like a weight was lifted from me. Whatever was in this water took these nasty things out of me and allowed me to breathe freely once again. This is how the renewal of our minds work. We sit down and fill ourselves with God's Word and take in things that are holy and pleasing to Him. At the same time, as we begin to soak in His presence and let His Spirit cleanse us, the evil things of the world begin to flee from us. The longer we stay in God's Word and soak in things of Him, the better we feel, the freer we feel, and the weight of the world that was holding us down from living out His truth gets lifted from us by the mighty hand of God. This enables us to breathe again and start living the life God has called us to. In this section of each chapter, we will examine how we might renew our minds and avoid falling for these methods the world uses to get us to accept the pattern of sin.

As a Christian, you know the only one that will truly give you hope despite what life may throw at you. The only true fulfillment anyone will attain in this life is when they are living a life filled with Christ. First and foremost, we have to remember that truth as Christians and never let anything or anyone make us lose sight of it. Whenever we fill doubt creeping its ugly head in, we need to think back to joy and peace Jesus has given us in life over and over again. Remember times like my story where you misplaced your hope and the feeling you were left with. Go back and soak yourself in God's Word and meditate on who Jesus is.

One of the best ways to keep your hope in Jesus when the world will tempt you to place it in anyone or anything else is to surround yourself with strong believers. When you have faithful brothers and sisters in Christ in your life to assure you in your hope and encourage you in your walk with Jesus, it becomes increasingly easier to remain faithful. God's Word tells us that when two or more are gathered in His name, He is in the midst of us. (Matthew 18:20) When believers unite together in Jesus' name, His Spirit is strong within them. The word synergy comes to mind. This is when one plus one equals three, four, or more. When people come together with the same mind, they are able to strengthen each other where they are weak and are able to accomplish unbelievably more than they could by themselves. While we are still in the flesh, we are weak, and every one of us has the temptation to fall back into our fleshly desires and doubt Who we put our hope in. We each have our individual weaknesses, but the powerful thing is that God did not create us all the same. Where you are weak, He has given another strength. So, when we come together as the body of Christ to encourage and support each other in our walks with Jesus, we are able to not only keep our hope in Jesus but grow in it.

"There is one body and one Spirit—just as you were called to the one hope that belongs to your call— one Lord, one faith, one baptism, one God and Father of all, who is over all and through all and in all. But grace was given to each one of us according to the measure of Christ's gift." (Ephesians 4:4-7, ESV)

The world, however, is lost and stuck in darkness, so we have to spread His hope throughout the world. We need to be a city set on a hill. When people see us, they should see the hope of Jesus flowing through our lives. This is a great way to truly love our neighbors by giving them hope, real hope, especially when they are in a very difficult situation.

We absolutely need to tell them of the most wonderful news that no matter what they have done, Jesus still died for them and is waiting with open arms for them to run to Him. He desires to give them peace beyond all understanding, love, and strength through whatever they are going through. He wants to be a friend to them, and more importantly, He wants to adopt them into His family forever. His love is unconditional, and the joy of the world sits in His hands. He is waiting to pour that out on each and every one of us; we just have to put our trust and faith in Him, and we will see him pour His joy out on us. The question, though, is what does it really mean to spread the hope of Jesus into the world?

An issue I see in our world is when Christians just tell people about the love and hope of Jesus without ever doing anything tangible to show it to those they are witnessing to, and that may not settle well with those people. We are called to be the hands and feet of Jesus. What good is it to tell people of the love, hope, and joy of Jesus and then leave them where they are, knowing you could have helped them? What does God's Word say about this?

"Then the King will say to those on his right, 'Come, you who are blessed by my Father, inherit the kingdom prepared for you from the foundation of the world. For I was hungry, and you gave me food, I was thirsty and you gave me drink, I was a stranger, and you welcomed me, I was naked and you clothed me, I was sick and you visited me, I was in prison and you came to me." (Matthew 25: 34-27, ESV)

"If among you, one of your brothers should become poor, in any of your towns within your land that the Lord your God is giving you, you shall not harden your heart or shut your hand against your poor brother, but you shall open your hand to him and lend him sufficient for his need, whatever it may be." (Deuteronomy 15:7-8)

Where I grew up a common phrase people would say when someone was going through a hard time was "I'll pray for you." I believe most people said this with a sincere heart, but how many of those people actually prayed with that person right then? How many forgot to even pray for them later in the day? I know I am guilty of doing this, and I regret it. Furthermore, how many people actually did something tangible to help that person asking for prayer when they had the time and resources to do so? This is kind of like if you were really sick and incapable of doing certain things and a friend calls you and says, "I'm here for you." At first, that sounds great and comforting, but what if you really needed help the next day and they never picked up the phone, and they did not come by to help you? Would you still think that person really cares about you? I doubt you would and in fact, you would likely be upset with them. The same is true when we only tell people that we will pray for them after they open their hearts up to us about needs they have in their life that we could have met. That person is likely not going to see that you truly care about them.

This is even more true of someone you do not know. My wife and I live right outside Nashville, and I regularly go to Nashville for work. Almost every day I could spot out where a couple of homeless people will be with signs asking for help. I know I have prayed for these people many times, but most days I just drive right on by. For a while, I thought, "well I said a prayer for them so at least I helped." We think that someone else will come along that can help them, and God will answer our prayer. How many times do we stop and consider that we may be an answer to someone else's prayer? Maybe God sent us in that person's direction today because He knew we had the time and resources to help them, and we blew it. We were too busy getting an extra thirty minutes of sleep in our beds while they were hoping to find a place to rest that night. We were too occupied with getting to work early to shoot the breeze with our friends when they just needed someone to say a nice word to them. If we just took the time some mornings or maybe every morning to talk with them, get out and pray with them, or give them some breakfast food or something that will help them, can you imagine the kind of outlook they would have on Christians then and more importantly on Jesus? If they knew Christians would go out of their way to help them, be kind to them, and be there for them when no one else would, they would know Christians truly care about them and show a love to people that the world does not. This is how you spread love and hope to those that feel hopeless.

Jesus calls us to go into the world and not only preach His Gospel but to live and breathe it. When someone encounters us, they will see a hope they have not seen in anything or anyone else, and they desire to know where you obtained it. I hear a lot of people say mean things about those that are homeless, those that are living a lifestyle that they should not, or those that are just different than how they may be. People say things like, they deserve to be where they are, or I am not associating myself with those people. My response to them would be two questions. Do you consider yourself a follower of Jesus? They will likely say yes, and my follow-up question would be: Jesus associated himself with sinners and outsiders all the time, so if you are following Him, why do you not do this? The reality is we do not want to do this because we do not want to get out of our comfort zone, but this is not a choice; we are called to this by Jesus.

This is how we spread His love and hope into the world. Of course, we share His word with them and what Jesus did on the cross, as Jesus is the only one that can save them from their sins, but if we do not follow what we preach, do you think people are really going to believe what you have to say? If you preach love and hope from

Jesus, but you neglect to show kindness and love to people you preach to, people will likely close their ear to you or view Christians in a negative light. Whether the person is homeless, living a sinful lifestyle, or just different than you, Jesus still died for them like He died for you. Nobody on this earth deserves the love of Jesus and His sacrifice on the cross. To Jesus, it did not matter that we did not deserve it, but what matter was that His love redefined our worth. Something that has stuck with me and challenges me to this day is the thought that when someone leaves an encounter with you, are they filled up with love, hope, and joy or are they left with sadness, bitterness, and malice? What is your life pouring into people today? Are you pouring hope and love into the world today by your actions and if not, what are you going to do to change that?

"We who are strong have an obligation to bear with the failings of the weak and not to please ourselves. Let each of us please his neighbor for his good, to build him up. For Christ did not please himself, but as it is written, "The reproaches of those who reproached you fell on me." For whatever was written in former days was written for our instruction, that through endurance and through the encouragement of the Scriptures, we might have hope. May the God of endurance and encouragement grant you to live in such harmony with one another, in accord with Christ Jesus, that together you may with one voice glorify the God and Father of our Lord Jesus Christ. Therefore welcome one another as Christ has welcomed you, for the glory of God." (Romans 15:1-7, ESV)

Staying Busy Keeps us from Living Out the Truth

Ring! Ring! This is the sound of another early morning. You reach over to hit the alarm and then, using all your willpower, you pull yourself out of bed. You rush to put on your dress clothes, fix your hair, brush your teeth, and run out the door. You jump into your car and begin to head down the road to work. Traffic is backed-up as is usual. You anxiously grip your wheel and grit your teeth as no one seems to want to let you over. You finally arrive at work and scurry into your desk to begin the day. You then spend the next eight hours glaring at a computer screen, typing away.

After work, you once again fight the traffic to get to your kid's soccer practice that night. You stay out till seven watching your kid practice and try to be encouraging to them although you are already exhausted. You get home and rush to cook dinner, so you can eat something before bed. You turn on the nightly news to see all the doom and gloom that occurred in your area over the last twenty-four hours. You then scroll through all your personal e-mails and check your social media for at least thirty minutes. After this, you may attempt to watch a show with your spouse or kid before getting ready to go to bed to start the entire routine over again the next day.

You think to yourself, "at least the weekend is approaching," only to be surprised with a million tasks that seem to flood your calendar. Not to mention your friends want to watch the big game together, there is a social party your spouse wants to go to, and your kids have a double-header soccer game. You stay busy all weekend long and before you know it Sunday night has come and gone, and Monday morning is here again.

This routine or one similar to it probably sounds very familiar to most people. We often times feel like we have to be the Energizer Bunny, but do not have the battery power to go with it. Cities seem to function twenty-four hours a day and there seems to be a never-ending list of things pulling you in every direction. We feel like rest is impossible. When we get home and finally get a minute of free time all we want to do is lay down or go to sleep. We have no motivation to go to church on Sunday mornings, no motivation to do a devotional, and no motivation to read our Bibles. If anything, we just want to sit and do nothing and watch a TV show or a movie.

In my own life, when I graduated with my undergraduate degree, I immediately started into my master's. Not long after starting my master's, I started working at a church part-time. It was a smaller church so some weeks I poured hours and hours into planning for new and upcoming events and trying to redirect the ministry in the way I felt God leading. About a month later, I begin a full-time job that required me to be in an office in Nashville five days a week. A few months after this, I got engaged to my beautiful wife Gracie. Needless to say, I was absolutely exhausted. At first, I managed pretty well. I was able to get everything done and still squeeze in time for family, friends and to prepare Bible studies. It did not take long, though, until I would come home from work fighting terrible traffic and want to do nothing but rest and sleep. I would be up till two or three in the morning working on papers. My relationship with Gracie suffered, and my spiritual relationship with God became a distant one at best. I was overwhelmed with how many things I had on my plate, and I was too full to include God on a daily basis. This was when I knew something needed to change.

I had to learn to that my relationship with God has to come first in my life and my relationship with Gracie has to come second. This was not possible with my current daily schedule. I knew that meant I would have to cut other things out; that is what I needed to do. I started to make certain days homework days and carve certain nights out just to spend with Gracie. I also tried to make time during my lunch break at work and throughout my day to prepare Bible studies, so I would not be up so late at night and could focus on my personal time with family, friends, and LORD. I had to learn to say no to some things to clear my plate up for the things that were essential to my physical and spiritual well-being. There are still many weeks I have to teach myself this same lesson as the world's tasks start to fill my plate too full.

See, this method of keeping people constantly busy is what the devil uses so effectively in America today to get people to turn away from God and start accepting the pattern of the world. He knows that if he can get you busy enough that your schedule is too full or you are too tired to go to church or spend time with God, then it will be easy to push you into following the world's pattern instead. You will begin to forget your former love and start loving the things of the world instead. You will be so consumed by everything worldly you have to do that it will start changing who you are and the fruit you produce.

"But I have this against you, that you have abandoned the love you had at first. Remember, therefore, from where you have fallen; repent and do the works you did at first. If not, I will come to you and remove your lampstand from its place unless you repent." (Revelation 2:4-5, ESV)

God commands us to rest. He valued this because we need time to rest and to reflect if we are to serve Him at our best and be at our full God-given potential. Our bodies were designed by God. When He designed each of us, He never designed us to constantly be on the go. He designed us to take time often to rest. If we ignore this, we not only go against God's design and command for us, but we also starve our minds and bodies of what they desperately need. He desired for us to spend time in meditation, prayer, fasting, and reflection. This gives our minds and bodies time to recover from the stress of the world and to reflect upon what we did and what we need to do going forward to serve Him the way He is calling us to. When we give into this method the world uses of being constantly on the go, we blatantly go against God's command and design for us. God made us in His likeness, and even God valued rest as an essential part of being. Look at what God's Word says all the back in Genesis.

"And on the seventh day God finished his work that he had done, and he rested on the seventh day from all his work that he had done. So, God blessed the seventh day and made it holy, because on it, God rested from all his work that he had done in creation."

(Genesis 2:2-3, ESV)

After God created the heavens and the earth and filled them, He took a day to rest and reflect upon what He had done. He did not rush into the next thing He could do, but took time to enjoy the moment and to take it all in. Many times in our lives today we have been so engulfed in the world's method of constantly being busy, that when we complete a task, we just run to start the next thing. Even as I was writing this, I was rushing through eating a pot roast my wife, and I worked hard on, so I could get back to writing. I had to stop myself, back away from the computer, and just enjoy my meal. I had urges throughout the meal to jump back on my computer, but I forced myself to slow down and just enjoy the moment. I actually enjoyed the pot roast much more this way and felt good about what we accomplished cooking together. We tend to never sit and enjoy what we just accomplished and what God did through us. We do not take time to reflect on what went well and what maybe did not go well so that we can grow from it. By rushing right into the next time, we miss the blessings in front of us. God wants us to live fully in the moment, and if our heads are always in the future, it is impossible to do that.

Many people likely think that humans have always been this way, but that is not true either. Sure, temptations were there to constantly be on the go, but the Jewish custom was to take a Sabbath every week. This was one day out of the week where the rested from all the stress of daily life. They reflected on what God had done through them, mediated, and prayed to God. They spiritually and physically renewed themselves for the next week ahead. Look at what God's Word says in Exodus.

"Remember the Sabbath day, to keep it holy. Six days you shall labor, and do all your work, but the seventh day is a Sabbath to the Lord your God. On it you shall not do any work, you, or your son, or your daughter, your male servant, or your female servant, or your livestock, or the sojourner who is within your gates. For in six days the Lord made heaven and earth, the sea, and all that is in them, and rested on the seventh day. Therefore, the Lord blessed the Sabbath day and made it holy." (Exodus 20:8-11, ESV)

What is important to note is that God's Word tells us that for six days, we should work, but on the seventh, we should rest. It does not tell us an exact date, but just that each person should find one day a week to rest and reflect. It also mentions that the entire family, including all servants of the person, should seek to rest on this same day. Why is that important? I think it is because God desires for the family to rest together one day a week to also renew and strengthen their relationship with one another as they renew and strengthen their relationship with God. Family life and spiritual life go hand and hand in many cases. Being constantly busy takes tremendous time away from being with our families, which in turn also hurts our spiritual life. God blessed us with a family for a reason, and this is part of our calling to love and cherish them. When we are constantly busy, we cannot do that or spend time with God. Thus we dramatically affect all relationships in a negative way.

Some people can interpret this day of rest as not being able to do anything at all. God's Word also addresses that issue. Life happens, and people get sick, and needs still come up. God still desires for you to take care of those that are sick as this is loving people and to help those you see in need. Look at how Jesus responded to those that questioned Him plucking heads of grain on the Sabbath.

"One Sabbath he was going through the grainfields, and as they made their way, his disciples began to pluck heads of grain. And the Pharisees were saying to him, "Look, why are they doing what is not lawful on the Sabbath?" And he said to them, "Have you never read what David did, when he was in need and was hungry, he and those who were with him: how he entered the house of God, in the time of Abiathar the high priest, and ate the bread of the Presence, which it is not lawful for any but the priests to eat, and also gave it to those who were with him?" And he said to them, "The Sabbath was made for man, not man for the Sabbath. So, the Son of Man is lord even of the Sabbath." (Mark 2:23-28, ESV)

Jesus wanted them to know that if someone is in need, whether it be they are hungry or something else, if we can help them and we feel God leading us to do so, even if it is the Sabbath, these are things we should do. We should not neglect those around us, especially in their time of need. We are called to love and serve others. However, if possible, we are called to spend the entire day in rest and reflection with our families. Why was it so easy for people to do this back then and so hard for people to do this today?

Although sin was very active in the world back then, most people in the Jewish culture still valued God's commandments. They desired to follow Him and live out what He had instructed them to do. They also did not have the kind of distraction that we do today. There were no television sets, there were no cell phones to constantly buzz for our attention, there were no neon lights covering the town so much they blocked out the stars, and there were no video games. There were plenty of forms of entertainment, but people also had a high value on God's Word and respected the fact that everyone needed to observe the Sabbath.

Today, we have sports on Sundays, big-time dramas every night of the week, twenty-four, seven fast food places and superstores, concerts, and more that constantly seek to pull our attention away from resting, meditating, and reflecting on God's Word. Our world today, for the most part, does not value God's commandments and people are living for themselves. They do whatever pleases them and feel good at the moment. We have bought into the lie of the world that the busier we are, the more successful we are. The more things we are involved in, the more socially acceptable we are. This is why our world today does not value rest, and because of this, people are getting pulled right into the pattern of the world.

How Do We Renew Our Minds?

The easiest answer would be to simply take things off your plate and spend more time with God and your family. Although I will talk about how we can do that, I also realize that our world is quite a bit different today than what it used to be, and many of our situations are very complex. Some of us work crazy hours or have multiple jobs because, without them, we would not be able to provide for our families. This is why I want to give each and every person, no matter their situation, some advice on how to take time to rest and to reflect.

The first thing we can all do is take time each day to journal things you notice God doing in and through. For example, one day I was working a job where I took orders most of the time, and the phone rang. Naturally, I assumed it was a person calling to place an order or ask a question about our policies or procedures. The company I worked for distributed Bibles all around the world and had lots of programs that people were involved in. To my surprise, the person on the other end of the phone was not a member, did not want to place an order, and did not have any questions about our policies or procedures. He simply found one of our Bibles in a thrift store and wanted to know more. I found out after talking to him that he was in a broken relationship and lost. He was looking for something that would truly fulfill him and knew there was something missing in his life. I was so surprised by this call and excited all at the same time that I had to try and keep my emotions in check.

I remember praying to God that He would help me through this conversation by giving me the words to say to this young man. Through His grace and love, I was able to lead him to Jesus. At the end of the conversation, the man expressed to me how much better he already felt and how grateful he was. He had begun a new journey in his life with the LORD, and that would last for all eternity. I wrote that date and that moment down in my phone, so when I had some free time, I could go back and remember how awesome of a thing the LORD did through me and reflect upon it. It is funny how we get so surprised when things like that happen to us, but in all honesty, we should expect things like that to happen to us all the time. When we are following the LORD, we will see Him open doors all the time in our lives. He will bring opportunities in front of us to help someone in need and maybe even lead them to Himself. So many times in life, we get caught up in the next task we have to do; we miss the open door right in front of us that God wants us to go through. There are people all around each of us that God has put in our lives to minister and witness to if we just stop what we are doing, look to Him, and follow His Spirit.

When we follow the Holy Spirit, we will see God do amazing things through us. When these things happen, make a note in your phone or, if you prefer to, write them down. Make a running list or notebook full of these amazing moments God has done through you. When you get a few hours to rest, you will be able to look back through your list or notebook and reflect on each of these moments. You will be able to thank God for each of them and be reminded of His hand upon your life and the ways He is using you.

Often times in our life we get so used to constantly going that it can seem impossible to shut our brains off. I know this happens to me all the time. I will come home from a stressful day and be anxious and fidgety all night long. My wife can attest to this as she has been woken up many nights by my tossing and turning or getting out of the bed. Even in moments where we are trying to rest, our minds may try very hard to think about everything else.

This is why having this list or notebook is so crucial. Even when we cannot remember in that moment what God has done in our lives recently because of all the junk that is floating around in our brains, we can look back at that list or notebook and be instantly brought back to those moments and begin to transition our minds to reflect on the things God wants us to.

Another great thing to do to get your mind in the habit of resting and reflecting more is to find an outlet to release all the stress and anxiety that builds up in you throughout the day. Like I said earlier, many days I come home fidgety and anxious, and I have a very hard time shutting my brain off from all the tasks I need to do that night or the next morning, and I miss the moments and blessings right in front of me. Many of you can probably relate as you come home from work, but you are not mentally home. You are not in the moment for your spouse and kids when they desperately need you.

What helps me and helps many other people is to find an outlet that you can release that stress and anxiety from work and life, so when you come home, you can be completely home physically, mentally, emotionally, and spiritually for your family. Running can be that outlet for me. If I can take ten to thirty minutes a day to run after work, I can tend to release a lot of stress and anxiety and be more relaxed and focused on my family when I get home. You have to find that outlet for you. Find something you can do at least ten minutes and probably no longer than an hour after work to release that stress and anxiety from work so you can fully be there for your family when you get home. If that is not possible, find something you can do a few times a week to help you relax. I have some good friends that go rock climbing every week. This is something that brings them happiness and helps them release all the stresses of the world for a time. My wife and I went with them once, and I think I slept better that night than in a long time from how exhausted I was.

Lastly, you need to seriously evaluate your life and everything you have on your plate. Sure, you need the meat and vegetables. These things may be things like your job, spending time with your family, and caring for the friend of yours going through a hard time. We often tend to make some things in our life, meat, and vegetables, when they are really desserts. These are things like going shopping every Saturday, attending every sports game of your favorite team, and going to that social event every Sunday afternoon. These things may be enjoyable, but these are not things you need in your life. If these things are causing your plate to be so full that Jesus and rest get put in the fridge to store away for later, there is a problem. Some of you may need to throw some of these items in the trash or store them in the pantry for an every now and then use, so you can make sure your time with Jesus has a secure place on your plate at all times and you intentionally include rest in your weekly schedule,

Many of us store up treasures for ourselves on earth. We feel like we have to do all things to be successful or socially accepted by all while destroying the things that are truly important in our lives. The question we have to ask ourselves is, are we living for the approval of man or the approval of God? We can be the most popular person on earth and the most successful in the world's eyes, but the world is fading away. What we do for our families and, most importantly, what we do for Jesus is eternal. Those treasures are stored up in Heaven and will be far more valuable than any treasure we can attain on Earth. What treasure are you storing up in your life today? If you do not have room for your family, Jesus, or rest, then what do you need to throw in the trash today, so you can make room for what is truly important once again your life?

Bradley Stubbs

Media Portrays Sin as the Right Way to Live

I want us to examine the pressure to accept sin from the media. I want to recap a scenario from a show my wife, and I enjoy watching. The show is about some young high schoolers and the lives they live trying to find their place in the world. There are many relationships throughout the seasons between the guys and girls, as is pretty accurate throughout high school. What troubled my wife and I, is after many episodes, we get introduced to these new characters that move to the town. That does not seem like a jaw-dropping plot twist, and it would not have been had the girl that moved not been homosexual or at least if the show would not have suddenly changed its plot to a girl trying to come out.

All of a sudden, this show that was about these high schoolers searching for their place in the world, the guys and girls dating one another, and all the drama that is involved in high school, now turned into several episodes of this girl seeking to be gay at this high school and accepted by everyone including her family for it. As the episodes progressed, we saw this girl get picked on at school, shut down by her older brother, and told she was wrong by her family. Then the show begins to portray this girl as a victim and goes so far as to have this new girl build a relationship with another girl on the show leading to her kissing this girl and then being told by the girl she kissed that she was not into that.

The show depicted the girl really upset that people did not approve of her lifestyle, and it made it appear that she could not be herself unless she was gay. She even said that this is who I am. The show worked really hard to build the plot up that the world was against her and that if they could just accept her lifestyle and encourage her in it, then all would be well. Otherwise, she could never live the life she was supposed to. The show at the end made a point of showing her friends and family come together to not only support her but to go on to encourage her to be gay as that is who she was, and they were wrong to not accept that at first.

There is something really important to note about this. My wife and I really liked this show, and we were really into the characters. We are both born-again Christians, and this show had both of us hooked. I am sure many other Christians around the country also were watching this show on a weekly basis. The show did not begin to air these episodes until probably thirty episodes in. Why is that so important? Because after thirty episodes, if you were regularly watching this show, then you were going to tune in the next week and likely watch all of these episodes as well because you enjoyed the overall plot of the series, and the show already had you hooked. You will likely think to yourself, "well, I guess I can make it through these episodes, so I can see what happens to the other characters after." This is exactly how the secular media will get into the minds of people, even and especially Christians. They will get you hooked onto something that is good and then mix in sinful material later on.

Your mind is already convinced the show is overall good, so when you see this sinful material on this show, your mind will also be tempted to register it as good. The media may also portray sinful lifestyles as who that person really is as they did in this show and that there is no way they could change the way they are living. They make it seems like they are the victims because some people in the world do not accept their lifestyle or their choice is not the popular one. They flip the boundaries of right and wrong and twist the mind of the viewer to make them question their own beliefs and make them feel bad for not accepting what the world is promoting as right.

In no way is it acceptable to make fun of, put down, or in any way be disrespectful to someone living a sinful lifestyle, but we are also called to lead them to the truth in love. As Christians, we know that living these lifestyles will never bring true joy or fulfillment, and I believe the media knows that too, but they will do everything they can to shut the truth out because they want the world to live the way they want to and one of the biggest ways is to start getting Christians to question their thinking when watching shows and movies like this. The more Christians question if their beliefs are truly right or if they are too strict or too tight about certain things, the less Christians will stand up against the world. The dimmer our light becomes, and the greater the darkness grows.

The media will portray someone living a sinful lifestyle as a hero if they come out to the world and stand up against what people traditionally thought was right. Think about this, when you watch a show, and they build it up to where the person living in sin stands up and challenges everyone to accept it; naturally, you start pulling for them. Your brain feels the emotion and the adrenaline of the situation and starts to convince you this lifestyle is something you should accept and even cheer for. Your mind can be easily deceived, and the secular media knows that. The devil is referred to as the master of deception. He uses shows, movies, and music to deceive us into supporting the things he does and that the world does, all while abandoning the things God's Word tells us to do.

Another way the media lures Christians into accepting sin as the way to live is by showing sin as the way the "popular" people live. These sinful lifestyles are the way to advance in the world socially. This is especially deadly in teens and young adults when everyone wants to fit in. We see commercials with all the "popular" people doing things that are sinful, movie and music stars that produce inappropriate material praised, and TV channels that frame people that oppose the world's views as outsiders, uneducated, or misguided. All humans want to be accepted by society, and when hormones are raging as a teenager, this is even more escalated. The devil knows this, and that is why we have seen such an attack on the younger generation in the last several decades.

The majority of males in the early twenties have likely watched pornography at one stage in their life if they are not still watching it. It is "normal" for middle schoolers and even late elementary kids to regularly say curse words that they hear from their favorite music singer, actor, or actress. Kids are acting like that because they are convinced by the world that these are the actions that will gain the approval of those around them and will bring them happiness in life. They believe that if they can act just like the people they see on TV and those they listen to on the radio, then one day they may be popular like they are.

I remember when I was in middle school. I had always grown up in church and knew right from wrong. I was not a very popular kid, as I will explain more later. I wanted to fit in with the world, and I was curious about the things I was told were wrong all my life because it seemed like all the popular kids at school were doing those things. I started to fill my mind with music, movies, and online sites that were not pleasing to God, but what seemed to make people happy in the world. These things were acceptable and encouraged by the world. To stand against these things almost seemed wrong, and that I was unloving toward people that chose to live these lifestyles. It was not long until the things I was filling my mind with started to change my attitude toward people and my life as a whole. This is because whatever we take in will eventually come out in our lives. Our thoughts control our actions, our actions control our lifestyle, our lifestyle becomes our character, and our character is who we are.

My desires started to change into more of what the world told me I should desire. I started seeing women in a different light than I had before. I started to believe that the "party life" or the "high life" the other kids were living was really was not that bad. I got involved in the wrong relationships and with the wrong friends not long after as I was also searching for the wrong things, but I was convinced that by accepting these behaviors and practicing these things, I would be fulfilled, or they would bring me happiness. The truth was that these things were exciting at first and gave me a sense of happiness in the moment, but that feeling wore off quicker and quicker the more I got involved with the wrong people and the wrong things.

I ended up feeling depressed and filled with guilt and shame. I had been consumed by the pattern of the world and believed the lie that if I accepted and lived out the things the world told us to, these things would bring me happiness and love. The complete opposite was the truth, and it took me a long time to recover from some of the mistakes I made. A big part of this started from what I listened to and saw from the media that was sinful but portrayed as a good thing that would bring me happiness, love, and joy.

The last big attack to conform to the pattern of this world from the media that I see rampant in our culture is the use of social media in a negative way. Social media can be a wonderful tool to connect with people we may not have been able to connect with otherwise. I use it on a daily basis to talk with family, friends, church members, and co-workers. The problem is just like everything else that God intends for good, the devil finds a way to perverse it. Thinking back on my childhood, the thing my mom told me to stay away from was Myspace. My childhood was not that long ago, and yet that seems like one of the least dangerous social media platforms out there in the world today. Social media is exploding at a rate never seen before, and new apps seem to be produced daily.

Again, most of these apps can be very good in what they offer to the world, but if we are not guarded, we will quickly get sucked into the pattern of this world through these social media apps. In the technologically advanced world we live in today, just by searching for things on the internet, people can track their interests. So, if a teenager searches for something innocent on the web, then the next time they get on a social media platform, the advertisements that appear may very well start showing inappropriate content because the internet believes this content is somehow related to what you searched yesterday. Please think about this example.

There was a guy that struggled with sexual immorality. He was trying to rid himself of this and wanted to change. One thing he was really passionate about was weightlifting. He looked up lots of weightlifting equipment websites and videos of famous weightlifters on his phone to further his development as a weightlifter. One day, he started looking on one of his social media apps, and there was picture after picture of fitness models, many inappropriate. He started looking at these advertisements more and more, and this begins to fuel that fleshly desire in him that he was working so hard to rid himself of.

He ended up going back down the path he was working so hard to rid himself of for quite some time. This led to many scars that still affect him today. Now, these advertisements did not make him do anything sexually immoral. What they did do, however, was warp his mindset to see women in the scandalous way he used to, and it fueled the fire of sexual desire within him. It brought him back to the life he used to live and built up a craving to go down that road again. I know several people that have similar stories to the example above. All of a sudden, everywhere they turn on social media, they are bombarded with inappropriate content that they never asked for simply because the internet thinks the content is something you would like. Their minds start racing a million miles a second. The longer they stay locked in on the inappropriate picture or video on the screen, the more they question the boundaries of right and wrong, and the more the fleshy desire starts to take over. This can be a tremendous stumbling block for some people. The scarier thing is that most people use some sort of social media for their jobs or to connect with people that they could not otherwise. So, the ones that stumble easily from this can, in a way, feel trapped in this unwanted cycle.

Although that can be very emotionally and spiritually draining, I think one of with not the most dangerous tools used from social media that I have witnessed from the young adults I have ministered to is the discover or explore feature on these social media apps. You likely know about this feature if you get on social media often, but if not, this feature basically shows what is popular around the world and pops up posts that the app suggests for you to look at or watch. I have seen teenagers fall into temptation and sin from looking at these explore or discover options day after day. Why is that? In the summer, what do you think the world likes to see? What do you think the fleshy desires in each of us desire? The world promotes very attractive men and women in skinny swimsuits or that are showing partial nudity. Many times, they are doing inappropriate things on videos. These posts get the most likes and comments because this is what the flesh desires, so they flood these explore or discover features on these apps. Other popular posts that I have also seen on these apps include people smoking weed, cursing left and right, and people doing dangerous things. These are the kind of things the flesh desires because outwardly, they look attractive or intriguing, and since the world is not following Jesus, people like and comment on posts like that far more than posts that are of morally good things. These posts rise to the top of everyone's discover feature, and it only takes one click to plunge headfirst into what the world promotes as right. To see what the world tells us will give us happiness and fulfillment. Look at what God's Word instructs us.

"Do not love the world or the things in the world. If anyone loves the world, the love of the Father is not in him. For all that is in the world – the desires of the eyes and pride of life – is not from the Father but from the world." (1 John 2:15-16, ESV)

The media knows that our eyes can very easily lead our minds and hearts in a certain direction. This goes along with what 1 John 2:16 says, "the desires of the eyes and the pride of life – is not from the Father but from the world." This is why we have to be cautious of what we take in or how much we take in. The more we consume things in the world, the more we will become like the world. The more we consume things of Jesus, the more we will become like Jesus.

How to Renew Our Minds

The more we watch and take in these sinful acts displayed on mainstream media, our minds start to convince us that these acts and "this language is really not that bad" and "we're being too strict." The truth of the matter actually is that when we start to not think of sin on TV and in music as wrong or not that bad, then we have gotten stale with God, and you need to watch out because a spiritual avalanche is about to start in your life, and it will try to pull down everything and everyone around you. What I mean by this is that when you start accepting that those sins portrayed on TV and in music as now okay or "not really that bad," then the devil has you exactly where he wants you because he has now convinced you that what the world says is okay is actually okay and that even though the Bible says different it does not really matter. Whether consciously or unconsciously, you have now moved from seeking God's Word for direction in your life to turning to pop culture to give you guidance on what is acceptable and not in life. When you have gotten to this place, the devil will begin to tempt you to take it even further until you are actually supporting the sinful things of this world and totally abandoning God's Word. Meanwhile, you will be tearing down everything and everyone around you, and this is when the avalanche of your spiritual life is in full swing.

I encourage that if this is you, to repent, to cleanse yourself from all impurities in your life, and begin to rebuild the foundation of your life on God's Word. Make your foundation in Jesus so firm and so strong that you when avalanches of sin are happening all around us, we will not be knocked down and swept away in them. However, we will still be standing firm in God's Word and shining a light into the world of darkness that is consuming so many others. Maybe for you, this means to watch and listen to more things that are holy and pleasing to God. For others, maybe this means that when shows have episodes like the one my wife and I watched, that you turn those off and you decide to not watch episodes like that, or for you, it may mean that if you see sin being shown in a positive light on these shows or movies, you find a different show or movie to watch. Most importantly, if you do decide to watch something that shows sin in a positive light, make sure you detox later and fill yourself again with the Spirit, so you will not begin to be sucked into your own spiritual avalanche

Also, be there for others when you see them start to go down this road or if the full-blown spiritual avalanche has already taken place in their life. Be there to pull them out of the rubble and mess they are buried in with love and truth and guide them back to the firm foundation that is in Jesus Christ. When the world comes to tear you down, point them to Jesus, who can lift them up out of the mess they are in and give them eternal life, the forgiveness of sins, and the joy and peace they desperately long for. One way to do this is to give them what I call the "small print" of their choices. When you watch commercials for certain medications, they always start with the positive effects and then at the end, they run through all the negative side effects that may take place in your life if you decide to take the medication. Most times, these possible side effects will be listed in small print at the bottom of the commercial as it is airing. Medication commercials do this because, by law, they are required to inform the users of all the potential bad side effects that may take place if they choose to use that certain medication. However, TV shows, movies, and music are not required by law to inform users of all the terrible side effects that may take place if someone decides to partake in things like sexual immoral acts, lying and gossiping, and partying till you drop. They make those things all appear to be the way to live, and there is no "small print" warning at the bottom. This is where Christians can really advocate for change in the world today in regard to media.

I have seen several students throughout my time in ministry that are struggling with sin many times with sexual sin. Their hormones are raging, and that pretty girl or handsome boy finally likes them. They start to go on dates, and if they find some time to be alone, it may seem almost impossible for them to resist doing something sexual with the other. Why is that? One, they are teenagers, and hormones are flaring, but there can also be self-control as many teens do abstain from having sexual relations until marriage. So, if that is not the reason, what is? I believe it is because as they were growing up and starting to understand sexual things better, sex was literally promoted everywhere for them. They saw it on TV, on social media, in the news, and the majority of teens have seen at least some form of pornography in this day and age.

The world has convinced them that this should be the goal in every relationship. If you can get the other person to have sex with you, then you have become as romantic and intimate with that person as possible, and now your relationship will be the best that it can be. To have sex with the other person is to show them you truly love them and are committed to them. So, when they get alone, and hormones start flaring, they both feel tempted to give themselves sexually to the other person because this is what the world has convinced them is how you show true love to the other person. I mean, you want them to know you love them and are committed to them, right? I think we would all agree that we want our relationship with our significant other to be the best it can be, so if sex is how we achieve that, why would we not do it? These are the questions that loom so heavy within the teen's head and even many adults in these romantic moments, so they accept what society deems is right, and they have sex with the other person. At this point, if society is correct, they should have the best possible relationship with each other and fall completely in love afterward. So, why do so many teens then come to a pastor, parent, teacher, or friend the next week in tears and completely broken because of what they did?

It is because no one told them about the "small print" side effects that would soon follow. Guilt and shame naturally fill both people because our conscience can sense what we did was not correct. Of course, many times, the young lady will later find out she is pregnant and now three lives have been forever changed. Most high school relationships do not work out, and once their boyfriend or girlfriend break-up with them, they feel as though the "system" did not work for them, and they must somehow be broken. They also feel like they just gave a part of themselves to someone they will now not end up with, and they can never get that back.

We need to remember that as Christians, we have to stand firm in God's Word and not be deceived by the world. Acceptance and love do not always go hand in hand. As Christians, we are called to love all people, but to also rebuke sin and lead people to the true cross of Christ. If a brother or sister is living in sin, it is not okay to accept their lifestyle because you are convinced that you are trying to show love from what you have heard on secular media. Rather, if you truly love that person and desire the best for them, you are to correct them in gentleness and truth, guiding them back to Jesus. You do this because you desire for them to receive the fruits of the Spirit and, most importantly, the forgiveness of their sins and salvation.

Another way to look at this is by comparing soda and water. My wife and I love Dr. Pepper, and we could likely drink three cans each day. Every time we drink that soda, it tastes good and even makes us feel good for the moment. The problem, however, is that if we each drink three cans in a day once that taste and "feel good" effect wears off, we will feel sluggish and probably dehydrated. The more days we continue this pattern, each time the drink still tastes good and makes us feel good while drinking it, but each night we always get that sluggish and dehydrated feeling. Furthermore, after a while, we notice that we have gained quite a bit of weight, can no longer do some of the things we used to do, get tired more easily, and are even having heart problems.

On the flip side, water to many people does not taste nearly as good as soda. We typically do not get some kind of "feel good" rush when drinking it. However, water has tremendous effects on every part of our life. I remember when I was running track in college. I had some great coaches that constantly poured into me. My coaches saw potential in me my freshman year, but I was not as strong of a runner as some of my teammates. I kept pushing myself at practice, and I saw minor improvements. My coach then told us one meeting to cut out all soda and to start eating healthier if we wanted to see maximum results. This was challenging for me because I was drinking at least one soda a day and eating chicken fingers and fries multiple times a week. I loved my coaches, though, and I wanted to be great for them and myself. I decided to make this change. I started drinking lots of water, juice, and Powerade. I ate salads for lunch and dinner, had sandwiches with ham and turkey, and ate a bunch of fruit.

Within a year, I went from a below-average runner to qualify for the Christian National Championship. I had never felt better in my life. I had a lot more energy, felt happier, and I was at my highest level of athletic performance I have ever been at. It was a real struggle many days because I did not like how difficult it was to drink more water and eat healthier, and it was not near as enjoyable, but the effects of doing that were well worth it. I can say that every time I have to drink a bunch of sodas throughout the day, I regretted it later, but I have never regretted the changes I made that year because the way I felt, in the long run, was unlike anything I had ever experienced.

The same is true with how the lost world views sin. Sin is like soda, and people know if they do these things that they will make them feel good at the moment, and every time they do them, they will still get this "feel good" feeling. The problem is that the long-term effects or the "small print" as I talked about earlier will be devasting. They will likely feel depressed, lonely, anxious, and empty like there is a void in their life. Following Jesus, however, is like drinking water. It will not always be the most attractive thing, it will be challenging, and the world will scream that if you follow Jesus, you will not have a happy or loving life, but nothing could be further from the truth. The "small print" of following Jesus is a life filled with hope, peace, joy, and above all, love from Jesus, and that love will pour out into every facet of your life. This is what Christians have to start sharing with people in the world. Yes, sin will taste good and give you that "feel good" feeling at the moment, but it will not last. Following Jesus will be difficult at times, but His love endures forever, and the fruits of the Spirit, you will begin to see in your life will give you joy that is constant. This is the "small print" we have to tell those that are deceived by what the world tells them will give them joy and love.

See, Jesus died on the cross for all people despite what lifestyles we were living and what gods we worshipped. Many people stop there and conclude that since Jesus showed unconditional love for all people despite what sinful lifestyles we were living in, then we should not tell others how to live and just love them despite what sinful lifestyle they may be living in. So often people in our society miss the fact that for anyone to receive the gift of salvation that Jesus made freely available to all, there has to be repentance of the sins we are living in. How can one follow Jesus but also still follow what is right in man's eyes? The truth of the matter is that there is no salvation without repentance. Thus one cannot be a follower of Jesus without repenting from the sinful lifestyle they are living. So, I urge each of us to love our neighbors with true Christian love being kind-hearted toward them, gentle but also redirecting them to the truth if you see them slipping away. This is the love we are called to show all people. This is the love that will change every aspect of their lives for the better and give them joy and peace that surpasses all understanding no matter what life throws at them.

"Preach the word; be ready in season and out of season; reprove, rebuke, and exhort, with complete patience and teaching." (2 Timothy 4:2)

"My brothers, if anyone among you wanders from the truth and someone brings him back, let him know that whoever brings back a sinner from his wandering will save his soul from death and will cover a multitude of sins."

(James 5:19-20)

Hate is a Strong Motivator

I am a fan of the *Star Wars* series like so many others. As I was recently watching one of the movies, I picked up on a key concept that runs so prevalent in our society. The concept is that hate is a motivator for us to conform to how society wants to live. Think about Anakin Skywalker and how he was taught from a very young age what was truly good and devoted his life to defending it as a Jedi. As he got older, the chancellor started trying to convince him that the Jedis were actually the evil ones and that they were trying to overthrow the government. He did this by consistently feeding Anakin with lies that what the Jedis stood for was actually evil. He convinced Anakin to believe that the Jedis were all about taking ultimate power for themselves and that they were holding others like Anakin back from experiencing all the power they could have. He also convinced him that they would never give Anakin the respect that he deserved. The chancellor later told Anakin that he was the chosen one and the one that should be in charge of the jedis. He claimed that the jedis knew this as well but because they personally did not like Anakin, they would never allow him to be the leader.

Over time Anakin became fueled with hate. The more hate he developed for the Jedis the more he begins to accept the mission of the dark side. Eventually, he became known as Darth Vader and is known as one of the worst Sith that the *Star Wars* universe has ever seen. Before Vader's death, he tells his son Luke that he was wrong to join the dark side. He admitted that hatred led him down this path and that he was deceived into believing he was supporting the right cause. He confesses that hatred is not the way to live. By the time Vader finally realized this, he felt that there was no hope left for him; he had traveled too far into the dark side and saw no hope remaining for himself. The truth of the matter is that the world uses this same concept today to persuade countless people to the "dark side".

What I mean by this is the world will try to get you to hate what is right, so you will follow what they believe is right, or in other words, for you to accept the pattern that the world wants you to accept. The world will twist and bend the truth to make it appear that Christians are the ones that are evil. People living in the world's pattern of sin will seek out Christians that have done terrible things and make it appear that all Christians accept and live out these horrific things. They will portray that Christians are holding people back from living out their true self or being who they were born to be. They will make people believe that Christians think they are better than anybody else, and if you do not follow the standards for living that Christians have, they will just view you as less.

Sadly, people that do not know the real truth are consumed with statements and ideas like this from the world and they begin to be fueled with a hatred inside for Christians and anything that has to do with Christianity. This hatred that forms inside of them grows as they truly believe that from what they see and hear from the world that Christianity is the evil side, so the opposing side must be the loving side. This leads people to accept whatever is completely opposite of Christianity and thus begins their transition to accepting the beliefs and mission of the "dark side" of the world. I see this very commonly with how the world will treat pastors and Christians that commit a terrible act compared to someone that is not a pastor or Christian that also commits a similar terrible act.

I want you to think about this example. If you ever watch the news and see a pastor from a church that has been accused of a major crime, it will likely be talked about for days. People will make statements left and right about the church, its members, and then eventually Christianity as a whole. People will take the horrible actions of one pastor, clergyman, or deacon and try and claim that this is how all Christians behave. The world will make claims that these actions are what all Christians teach and practice. People that are not Christians hear these rumors going around and start to build a hatred for Christianity as they think these actions are what all Christians must promote when in reality, the complete opposite is the actual truth. If they are not guided to the truth quickly, their hatred will likely grow so much against Christianity that whatever Christians stand for in the future, they will automatically stand against it even if it is clearly the wrong choice.

I have met people who believed they could not leave their kids in a church nursery because they had heard of pastors inappropriately touching children. This really troubled me. I am fully aware that this horrible behavior has happened in churches, but to think all churches behave like this, how did that thought occur? It likely happened over years of media coverage skewing the truth and people filling society's mind with false statements about Christianity and the Church. See, every time a church had an incident like this, people talked about it. After a few instances occurred, the world warped people's minds into thinking this was a common occurrence and a pattern in churches across the country. People that did not know the truth likely believed most pastors are secretly pedophiles.

If ten churches across the country had instances like this that made the news and people spread the word, even though that was likely ten churches out of the thousands and thousands of churches across the country, this was enough evidence for the world to grab hold of this idea and convince a countless number of people to believe the idea that all churches are a threat to children's safety. They convinced people that they should stay away from anything to do with Christianity as that is what is truly evil. The world made it seem that you should be ashamed to bring your child into a church as you are doing something evil.

Clearly, for any church pastor or anyone for that sake, to do anything like this is a horrible tragedy and there should be consequences, but why does it seem like the world attacks the church more on things like this than other organizations?

We may be tempted to think it is just because pastors are held to a higher standard, but I do not think that is the whole story. Think about all the sexual assault stories that have come out about coaches and trainers, and we do not see hardly anyone telling people to avoid playing sports or that all sports organizations are evil. Why is that? I believe it is because the world does not want people to follow God because that is vastly different from how they choose to live. The world wants people to play sports and do things that take up their free time because those things do not lead people to stand up against the pattern of living the world promotes. Whereas, if people start going to church and really taking in God's Word, they are likely to change the way they live from conforming to the pattern of the world to transforming their minds. This would lead to people standing against what those in power in this world believe.

The world does not want that, so if they can make people believe church is dangerous and evil, it will spark hate within people. This will ultimately lead people to avoid going to church and continue to follow the pattern of the world. They will do this because they think truly believe that they are doing the right thing by not endangering children or whatever the claim may be. They figure by following what the world says is right they must be supporting the right causes and loving people. This is how the devil uses hate to keep people continuing in the pattern of the world and away from God's Word which will transform their life and give them true joy, peace, and hope.

How to Renew our Minds

First and foremost, we have to make sure that as Christians we are living above reproach. It is unacceptable and disappointing to have pastors and congregants living in sin within and outside of the church. We are all going to make mistakes, but someone living a life truly changed by the Gospel of Jesus Christ should not fall into such sins as the ones mentioned above. Falling into such sins is not only wrong and disrespectful to Jesus but will almost undoubtedly completely lose that person's witness to the world for a long time. In addition to that, it will also hurt the witness of every other member in the body of Christ.

I believe there is forgiveness for the worst of worst sinners, even those that are pastors or regular church attenders from our LORD and Savior Jesus Christ. The problem is not that Jesus will never forgive these people or even that Jesus will not use them again in the future to do things for His kingdom because I believe that He will if they ask forgiveness and repent. The issue is that the world that does not follow Jesus may not be so forgiving, and the world has a bad habit of labeling groups of people from a handful's actions. That is why, as Christians and especially Christian leaders, we have to do all we can do to live fully surrendered to Christ and, by doing so, not leave ourselves open to evil accusations whether they are true or not. Once accusations start flying around about Christians in a negative light, it will not be long until the world catches on, twists the truth, and tries to use those accusations to fuel the fire of hatred that people will begin to have for Christianity.

One of my favorite stories I have been told is of Rev. Billy Graham. He was a wonderful evangelist and led a countless number of people to our LORD. One day he was about to get on an elevator when the doors flung open and all that stood there was a woman staring back at him. He saw no one else trying to get on the elevator, so he informed her that he would wait for the next one. Some people may have seen that behavior as rude, but this was a common behavior from Rev. Graham. Someone witnessed this and eventually asked him why he was doing this. He responded by telling them that if he ever sees a woman by herself on an elevator and he is the only one about to get on, although he knows he is committed to his wife and would never do anything on purpose to harm their marriage, he did not want to put himself in a situation where accusations could be made about him that would in any way harm his witness for the LORD and his marriage with his wife.

He did not want even to take the chance of anyone, whether it be that woman or someone else, to come back and accuse him of doing something with that woman while they were alone behind closed doors on the elevator. He cared about his witness to the world for Jesus Christ, and he knew that if any accusation like that were to come out against him that it would damage his witness to the world, and people may not receive the Gospel because of it. He also valued his marriage and did not want to do anything that could cause tension between his wife and himself. He refused to let these things happen, and that is why he is still considered one of the greatest evangelists of all time. He was able to reach a countless number of people for Jesus. This is what it means as a Christian to live above reproach. It means you consciously think about your actions and words and before you say something or do something. You make sure that by saying or doing that action or speaking those words, your witness for Jesus Christ will in no way be damaged.

Next, we have to make sure that people see the love of Jesus within us. The lie that acceptance of the world's beliefs equals love for others will only be uncovered when people in the world see unconditional love coming from Christians. A love they have never seen before that is so intriguing to them that they must find out how Christians have attained this. If people see that kind of love within believers, they will realize the "love" the world promotes falls majorly in comparison to the love given by the Father. Christians will shine a light in the world on what the true right side is.

Football was and is a big deal in the South. I know as a kid, I would study what was going on with my favorite football team more than God's Word throughout the week. After years of investing week in and week out into supporting my favorite team, I had grown a love for them. I was so passionate about that team and wanted to see them be the best they could. Every time they took field, I wanted to see them win. Because of the nature of sports being extremely competitive, I begin to despise any team that could possibly get in the way of my team being the best. Over time, the molded into a hatred for the other teams, especially the ones that were the biggest threat to my team being the best.

I remember I had a realization one week when my team was playing another for the championship. The head coach we had was cursing at the players, other coaches, and referees. I sat in my house watching this take place as the opposing team's coach was encouraging his players, talking about Jesus at press conferences, and was carrying himself in a respectful manner. I stopped and a feeling of shame entered into me. I had said some terrible things about this team in the past and in a sense, developed a form of hatred for them all because they were not the team I was cheering for. In reality, this team was likely following God more than my team was, and they behaved in a much classier way. What if by them winning the game, Jesus' name would be professed to the millions watching? Should I not desire for that outcome far more than the team I chose to cheer for to win? Sure enough, after the opposing team won the championship, the coach praised the name of Jesus in front of millions watching from home. A sense of joy filled me and made me realize how much I had let myself get sucked into the pattern of the world.

If we are filled with hatred, whether it be from sports or something else, we will become blinded as to how we should be living and who or what we should be supporting. We will lose sight of being the people God has called us to, and love will not flow from our mouths. Our mouth is a heart monitor. What is built up on the inside will come out at some point. If we have any kind of hatred with us, it will likely come forth through our words and actions, if not right away, in the future, and can ruin our witness to the world.

The best way to show the kind of love Jesus calls us to is by first and foremost making sure we are filling ourselves with His love daily through reading His Word and spending adequate time in prayer. The next is to think about how Jesus would respond to the world's hatred today by His words and actions. When our blood gets boiling over something as small as a football game not going the way we want it to or something as large as someone insulting us, do we respond the way Jesus would? Do we instead curse at the TV, spur an insult back at that person, or display hatred in our body language? A good test all Christians face is when the world makes terrible accusations about other Christians whether true or not and these make big time news, how do most Christians respond? Sadly, I feel like many of them are quickly filled with anger and immediately go on social media to post an ugly post about the person or party that claimed this.

They will accuse that person of lying, being evil (and that is one of the nicer things people tend to say), or if the accusation comes out to be true, they will say things like, well, these people did x, y, and z, so they have no right to hate on Christians for doing x, y, and z. The truth of the matter is that when Christians respond back to the world's hatred with hatred of their own, it just fuels the fire of hatred in the world today and gives people in the world that now have a bad view of Christians an even worse view. It also very likely may confirm in these people's minds the fact that Christians are the evil ones and the ones on the "dark side."

Think about Martin Luther King, Jr., and all that he accomplished. People hated African Americans just for the simple fact that they were African American. They would take the actions of some African Americans and claim that all African Americans were violent, rapists, or a danger to society, and people should keep their children away from them. Sound familiar? This is clearly wrong, just like the world today tries to say the same kind of things about Christians today and will sometimes base their claims on what just a handful of bad Christians did. Martin Luther King, Jr. was also a pastor, and one thing he learned that changed the way the country began to see and treat African Americans is the concept that you cannot fight hate with hate. You must fight hate with love. He led many peaceful protests where he would encourage those protesting with him to not respond back to the violence and hatred being shown to them in the same way, but to keep marching forward in peace and to show kindness to those around them. He knew that if they were to start being violent to those showing hatred against them that it would only confirm in these people's mind the ideas they already had about African Americans.

He knew that if people could instead see African Americans as the victims, as the ones remaining peaceful and loving despite the hate being shown to them, that they may have a change of heart about what kind of people most African Americans were. This concept changed the country and also lead to a very successful Civil Rights Movement.

The same can be said about Paul in the New Testament. Paul faced lots of persecution from the Roman government that hated Christians. The Roman government saw Christianity as a threat to their government and the power they had, so they tried to convince the whole nation that anyone that holds the beliefs of Christians should suffer punishment and is a disgrace to the government. One day Paul and Silas were encountered by a slave girl who was possessed. They stopped and helped this poor girl by casting the demons out of her and setting her free. They committed a great act of love for this girl that they never before this encounter. You would think the people that witnessed this would be so proud of Paul and Silas for doing what was right and in turn, show love back toward Paul and Silas, right? Well, that is not the world they lived in then, and that is not the world we live in now as when her owners saw that their way of profit was gone, they ordered the magistrates to seize Paul and Silas. Paul and Silas were actually beaten with rods for casting the demons out of the girl and then thrown into prison with shackles put on their feet.

At this point, most people would be so furious because they did everything right, yet they were told they were in the wrong, got beaten, and put in prison. What is so important for us to note is that Paul and Silas' joy did not come from their circumstances, but from the LORD alone. They knew in their hearts they were in the right and that these people were lost. How else do you expect lost people to respond? Why should they expect non-believers to respond how believers would respond? Paul and Silas also knew that if they were to lash out against these people it would only further build their hatred toward Christians and that it would then give these people a "reason" to be against the Christians.

So, how did Paul and Silas respond to all this undeserved hatred toward them from the world? They responded with the love of the Father. With true undefiled, no strings attached, love. They started singing hymns to God while in prison. This was so contrary to the norm that everyone in prison was intrigued and inspired by the joy these men had after facing terrible persecution and hatred. All of a sudden, an earthquake shook the prison cells and opened all the cell doors up. This was Paul and Silas' chance to escape and live free again as the deserved all along. So, they sprinted out of jail, right?

Actually, Paul and Silas stayed in the prison cell they did not belong in, and because of their faith and joy in the midst of this terrible circumstance, they convinced every other prisoner to stay in their cells as well. Why was this so important? The jailer that held them in this prison had fallen asleep and was about to kill himself when he woke up and saw the jail cells all broken open, thinking the prisoners had escaped. He knew that the Romans would kill him if they knew the prisons escaped on his watch, and he decided to take his own life instead. When Paul cried out for the jailer to stop because all the prisoners were still there, he not only stopped from killing himself, but he was so amazed by these men that he listened to what Paul and Silas had to say. He gave his life to the LORD and then went home and told his entire family and every one of them received salvation that night because of the unconditional love of God they witnessed through Paul and Silas. Love defeated all the hate that was shown toward Paul and Silas that day, and it overpowered hate so much that an entire family's eternity was changed. If Christians today showed that same love toward the world when the world shows tremendous hatred toward us, imagine the impact on the Kingdom of God we can have!

The Devil will use Knowledge to Conform

One thing I see with a lot of people in America especially is the strive for knowledge. We commonly believe that knowledge is power, and there is this desire that is growing in people across the globe for power and importance. There is a huge emphasis on getting degrees and being the smartest one in your field. The devil is well aware of this, and just like anything else that is intended for good, he will do everything he can to turn it into something evil. Think back to the very first humans, Adam and Eve. What did God tell them not to do? He told them not to eat from the tree of Knowledge of Good and Evil. What did Satan then do? He tempted Eve to eat from the tree because he claimed that God was just afraid of them gaining that knowledge because they would become as powerful as He is. Sure enough, Eve ate from the tree and then gave some to Adam to eat as well. This was the first sin in the world, and although Adam and Eve had knowledge, they would find out very quickly that their knowledge would never come close to equaling that of God's. They were separated from God and evil surrounded them. They became ashamed and lost the joy they had.

Unfortunately, the devil still uses this same method in our world today as the lie that once you gain enough knowledge you do not need God, floats all around us. Day after day people still fall victim to this method and that is why it is so important for us to talk about it. The world we live in today challenges us to only believe in what we can see and what makes logical sense in our minds. The world will tell us that some events in the Bible are impossible because we do not see those same events occurring today or that in our human minds those events could not be logical. This thought process puts the human brain's ability on the same scale as God's and claims that anything that does not make sense in our brains must be flawed. This is not a new thought process as we can once again go back to the Garden of Eden and see that Adam and Eve thought the same thing. They believed that if they ate from the tree of Knowledge of Good and Evil that they would become as smart as God.

Today, people do not eat from a tree of Knowledge of Good and Evil, but they do discover new things all the time. We have advanced so much scientifically and technologically over the last few decades that it is truly astounding. The devil knows this as well, and he tries to convince the world that because of all of these new discoveries and new technology humans have discovered or invented, that we no longer need God or that somehow, we have outsmarted the Bible. The world constantly feeds us the lie that we should now use science as our sole source for how the world was created, how people were made, and how we should live. This lie from the world that humans are all-knowing quickly begins to bleed into all areas of life. People believe that we should use psychology alone to treat people with mental struggles, and we should only trust medicine to heal the sick. The world will claim that God does not understand those things because when the Bible was written, people did not have access to the kind of knowledge we have today, and since we now have these tools, we should only use them and ignore the outdated advice in the Bible.

There is nothing wrong with science, psychology, and medicine to help us improve our lives and the lives of those around us. I think God calls us to this as He is the one who gave us the minds to think about these things and the materials to form and build the things that we have.

The problems arise when people start to push God's Word out and replace it with human reason and knowledge. People tend to act upon what they know and see in today's realm and trust human reason alone, rather than trust the One that can see all.

It is sort of like God is in the press box of our lives. He sits in heaven watching over us and can see exactly what life is about to throw at us, just like a coach in the press box can see what the defense of the opposing team is about to throw at the offense. The offensive coordinator in the press box may be able to tell that the opposing coach just called a corner blitz. The quarterback, however, with his limited vision of the field, may not have been able to see that call come in. Instead, the quarterback sees a relatively spread-out field and thinks he will have plenty of time in the pocket. Thus, it would be perfect for a pass play. The offensive coordinator rushes to inform the coach on the field to call a run up the middle. The coach yells out at the quarterback to change the play to a run down the middle.

The quarterback, however, thinks to himself, the coach must not know what he is talking about because he can clearly see the defense is set perfectly for a pass play. He knows he has studied the film, and he knows when he sees the defense line up this way exactly what the players are going to do. Because the quarterback believes he has all the knowledge he needs to make this play successful, he ignores the coach and snaps the ball. He turns right, looking at his star receiver with anticipation, just waiting for him to break on his route. He is so eager to let the ball go and gain a big pass play down the field when suddenly, BOOM! A crushing blow comes in from his blindside from the blitzing corner he never saw. He loses the football on impact, and the opposing team recovers. As he is on the ground, he thinks to himself how he could have missed that when he was so sure he knew what the defense was going to do. Sadly, this is the same thing many of us do in our lives today.

Many of us look at what we can see directly in front of us with all the technology, psychology, and tools at our disposal and make the most reasonable choice we can make, thinking we have all the knowledge we need. We use our education and experience in this world alone to respond to situations and questions that arise in our life. The issue is whether we want to admit it or not, our knowledge is very limited. How many times did you make the most logical and educated choice about something and then get slammed in life by that blitzing corner? This is because no matter how hard we try, humans will never have the knowledge to see exactly what will happen in the future or to know every detail of what happened in the past. Adam and Eve learned this concept the hard way, and many people do and still will learn this concept the hard way. Only God, who sits high above us and is all-knowing, can give a perfect account of every event in the past and can know exactly how every decision and choice we make will affect the rest of our lives.

This is why we have to seek God's will in every choice we make. He is the only one that can tell us what the best choice will be every time because He knows how that will affect you and those around you in a positive way in the future. If you stop and think today, with all our technology and educational advances in this world, not a single person can tell you what will happen to them on this day five years from now. So, when you make a decision today, the world may tell you that the choice you are about to make is the most logical and educated one, but if you feel that God is telling you to choose differently, then listen to the voice of God, who truly holds all knowledge and wisdom. He will guide you to make the choice that when you look back on this day five years down the road, you are proud of. When that blitzing corner comes to hit you in life, you will be able to dodge him and make the big play downfield and look up at your "coach" with a grateful heart.

How to Renew Our Minds

We have to stop putting so much trust in the knowledge the world gives us and put more trust in the knowledge of God's Word. Here is what I mean by that. Before Gracie and I got married, we went to a pre-marriage counselor for over two months. We were assigned a workbook to work through together, and we had about an hour each week to talk with the therapist about what we tried, what worked, and what did not. She would then give us some tips to help us in areas where we struggled and some ways to continue to strengthen the areas we had done well in. This was extremely helpful for us, and we still use many of the techniques we learned in those sessions today. We also went through weeks of pre-marriage counseling with our pastor. This was also extremely helpful and helped prepared us for the journey we were about to embark on.

The key thing in each situation was that both of these people were Christians, and we had high confidence that they would stay firm in God's Word. Thus, they would not tell us to do anything that would contradict God's Word. One person was not in ministry and had tons of knowledge of psychological techniques; the other was in full-time ministry and had tons of knowledge of God's Word and also real-life experience counseling many different kinds of couples. So, they used their knowledge of the world and God's Word to teach us very powerful and helpful tools.

Unfortunately, many couples do not have the same experience. They may get told that physical intimacy would help the relationship, so they get sexually involved before marriage. They may be encouraged to move in together to see how the transition goes before they get married. Other counselors may tell clients to act upon the homosexual desires they are having because that is who they truly are. They may encourage someone to partake in other sinful acts because they have been proven to increase happiness, or they have some other benefit that goes along with it. They back these claims up with studies done by various people in the world.

Do you see the contrast? A therapist that is deeply rooted in God's Word will also give advice based on research and studies done by various people around the world, but the difference is that they will not encourage a client to do something that contradicts God's Word. Therapists that are not Christians or those that very much oppose the Christian beliefs may encourage clients to live lifestyles contrary to God's Word and will use their knowledge from the world to convince them that what they are telling them is the best or only route for them. See, studies can be flawed, and data can be skewed.

More than likely, sinful practices will bring pleasure to a person for a short time, but they will not fulfill them. Living a sinful lifestyle and doing whatever you want to do may seem thrilling and free for a while, but it will never truly fulfill a person or heal them. This is why so many people that are living in sin feel like they are still missing something and end up in deeper depression and struggle with anxiety. The saddest part is that these people that do not know if they are living in sin or not are convinced that their lifestyle is just who they are, and they must accept that so they can truly find love and/or love themselves. They believe this because someone with knowledge on the subject encouraged them in this way. The truth, however, is that by accepting the sinful lifestyle they are living in they will never find true peace and love within themselves and they will not be able to love others the way God calls us to.

If you have a bunch of knowledge from the world and you are a Christian, then you have a tremendous opportunity. You can speak truth to those searching for answers and give them not only knowledge that can help them in what they are going through, but knowledge that will change their life for the better. You have the tools to make a great change in the world using the knowledge you have obtained from it, but at the same time, when you also stand firm in God's Word, you will be able to witness to a countless number of people.

In order to obtain knowledge of God's Word, you have to be in His Word. This means that you do not just go to church on Sunday, hear the pastor preach, and think to yourself you did your best to learn God's Word that week. God's Word should be something that you read and study daily. It is very similar to eating. If I go half a day without eating, I will start feeling weak and probably a little irritable; if I go two days or more without eating, I will be sick at my stomach and so weak I will not feel like doing anything. The longer we go throughout the week without studying God's Word, the weaker we will feel spiritually, and the more we will deprive our souls of the knowledge we need. We may be tempted to say and act in ways we should not because we lack the wisdom to respond to people the way God calls us to.

I know for me personally; I have a few personal devotions I try and do each day in addition to preparing Bible lessons each week. If I skip a day or more, I can feel myself getting spiritually weaker and distant from God. God desires to be in an intimate relationship with each of us. The way we grow in our relationship with God is to spend time with Him and learn more about Him. We can only do that if we have a spiritually healthy prayer life and value time in God's Word as an essential part of our day. If I were to go days without talking to my wife and showed no interest in learning more about her, we would have a rocky marriage, to say the least. I would also lack the wisdom to know how I should act and respond in various situations that would be pleasing to her. The more I learn about my wife and spend time with her, I pick up on how she expects me to respond when different things happen. I learn how she desires for me to respond to certain events that will show her the most love and respect. The same is true in our relationship with God. The more time we spend in His Word, and the more time we spend with Him in our prayer time, the better we will know how to respond to certain events in the world, and the better we will be able to serve and please Him.

Although knowledge is a wonderful thing and we should strive to attain it, another thing we need to consider is that if we have all the knowledge in the world and no desire to use it to change the lives of others, we are as good as a textbook buried on a shelf. Your knowledge should prompt you to act and respond in a certain way to impact the lives around you in a positive way. If you have spent time with God through prayer and studying His Word and have been blessed with knowledge and wisdom from Him, then use that in a powerful way for His Kingdom. Be able to go into the world and defend the truth and speak in an intelligible way about difficult topics and challenging questions posed by the world. Take the knowledge you have and live it out in all you do.

One of my favorite stories in the Bible that applies so well in this is the story of the Good Samarian. I learned something recently about this story, that gave it a whole new meaning to me. Look at what God's Word says in Luke 10:25.

"And behold, a lawyer stood up to put him to the test, saying, "Teacher, what shall I do to inherit eternal life?"" (Luke 10:25, ESV)

As this story begins, a lawyer decides to test the knowledge of Jesus. Many of us, including myself, have likely read that story and pictured the kind of lawyer we are used to today. A person that is standing in the courtroom pleading their case in front of a judge and jury. This, however, was not the same type of lawyer this story is referring to. This man was likely an expert on the Levitical law of the day. He knew the Word of God better than most and possibly better than anyone else that lived around him. He thought he knew more than Jesus and decided to test him in front of others to show those watching that he was more knowledgeable.

Jesus answers this lawyer by asking a question back to him. Jesus asks the man what was written in the law and what was his reading of it. (Luke 10:26) The lawyer replies back, "You shall love the Lord your God with all your heart and with all your soul and with all your strength and with all your mind, and your neighbor as yourself." (Luke 10:27, ESV) Jesus responds to him by telling this man, "You have answered correctly; do this, and you will live." (Luke 10:28, ESV) At this point, Jesus has answered the lawyer and even confirmed him, in that this man knew the right answer and was knowledgeable. You would think this would be the end of the story, but the lawyer still is not satisfied. God's Word then says, "But he, wanting to justify himself, said to Jesus, "And who is my neighbor?" (Luke 10:29, NKJV) The lawyer thought he could really show off his knowledge on this, but the story Jesus then tells this man shows us just how little our knowledge compares to

God's and also gives us insight into how we are to respond with the knowledge we have attained.

Jesus responds to this lawyer by telling him a story. He tells us a certain man that went down from Jerusalem to Jericho and fell among thieves, who stripped him of his clothing, wounded him, and by the time the thieves departed him, the man was half-dead. After some time, a priest and a Levite journeyed down this same road. As they approached the man, they went to the other side of the road and continued on their journey, leaving the man where he was. Now, a Samaritan also found himself traveling down the same road, but as he approached the man, he did not go to the other side of the road as the two men before him but had compassion for the man. The Samaritan bandaged his wounds, pouring on oil and wine, he set the man on his own animal, brought him to an inn, and took care of him. The next day, when the Samaritan departed, he took out two denarii and gave them to the innkeeper, saying, "take care of him and whatever more you spend, when I come again, I will repay you." (Luke 10:30-35, ESV)

After telling this story, Jesus asked the lawyer who was the neighbor to this man who fell upon thieves. The lawyer responds to Jesus by saying it was the man who showed mercy on him. Jesus then tells this lawyer, "Go and do likewise." (Luke 10:36-37, ESV)

In this story, there is a very important lesson that I looked over for years until someone brought this to my attention. This lawyer had more knowledge of God's Word than probably anyone else in the area, yet as Jesus was pointing out to him, he was missing the point. It is great to have knowledge in God's Word, and as I talked about earlier, we should be trying to grow in our knowledge of who God is daily, but our knowledge of God is basically pointless if we never use it in the world. It is a great thing to know about mercy and compassion for others, but if you never show mercy and compassion upon others, then your knowledge is useless. Jesus was telling this lawyer that he needs to now go and live out the things he has learned. The same is true for us. Many of us have lots of knowledge of God's Word but are not living it out in our lives.

The devil has made us master of excuses. See, the road from Jerusalem to Jericho was a dangerous road. As we can see from the story Jesus told, the man was robbed and nearly beaten to death. This was not an uncommon occurrence on this road. Many of us today that are ministers, prominent Christians, and has lots of knowledge of God's Word would pass by people in desperate need on the side of the road if they were in a bad area of town or in a dangerous city. We would just sit in our nicely heated cars and drive on by. We would say things like we are too busy to stop or we would not be able to really help. The truth is we have stored God's Word on a shelf in our brains and have locked the door on our hearts so His Word never gets stored where it should. We have all this head knowledge of what it means to be a Christians, but a true follower of Jesus hides God's Word in their hearts that they may not sin against God, and so His Word will change every aspect of who they are. They will begin to say, think, and act in the way Jesus would. They would truly be a neighbor to all they come in contact with, and when they share His knowledge with others, those people will listen because they know the person that is telling them these things does not just know and believe them, but they live and breathe them.

If you keep all your knowledge to yourself for your benefit alone, when you leave this earth, the story God has given you and all the knowledge you have obtained may just get buried on a shelf and collect more dust as the years go on. The disciples spent years walking with Jesus attaining all the knowledge they could, and after all these years of attaining knowledge, what was the last thing Jesus commanded them to do before He left Earth? He said, "All authority in heaven and on earth has been given to me. Therefore, go and make disciples of all nations, baptizing them in the name of the Father and of the Son and of the Holy Spirit, and teaching them to obey everything I have commanded you. And surely, I am with you always, to the very end of the age." (Matthew 28: 18-20, NIV) Jesus told them to now GO...GO into the world and share all that you have learned from Jesus with the world and make disciples for Him. Teach the world the truth and do it in a way that honors and pleases God.

We are called by Jesus to share our knowledge of Him with the world around us and make disciples for Him. If our lives are like books, we are not meant to gain all the knowledge we possibly can just to stay on the shelf; rather we are meant to take all the knowledge we have inside of us and open up our stories to the world for the world to read our lives and see the hope of Jesus Christ in us. God is calling each of us to take our stories and share them with the world around us. This may mean simply going next door or, for some, maybe going across the globe, but God has called each of us to share the knowledge of Him within us with the world around us. We have a chance to truly be a neighbor to each and every person we come in contact with. If there are people in your life, God has put them around you for a reason. We each have the choice to be a light to them, sharing the greatest truth they will ever hear or to leave them in more darkness than they were before they encountered us. Do not arrive in Heaven having to face Jesus, and He looks into your eyes and ask you why you did not share His Word with those He called you to, or why you did not take the time to talk with someone He called you. Never find yourself too busy living for yourself or too scared to stand up against the world. We need to remember that if God is for us, then who can be against us?

The most blessed people in the world are those that are living for God not themselves and have opened the story of their lives (which is ultimately is His story) to the world around them, truly being light into the world of darkness. You may be scared to open your story for the world to read and I understand that as I was once very scared for the world to read my story especially a few chapters, but when your story centers around the redeeming love of Jesus Christ, Jesus will use every chapter for His glory. The safest place you will ever be on this world is right in the center of God's will. Are you living a life of comfort today or the life you are called to live? I encourage you to put down the things you are doing in living for yourself and start doing the things God is calling you to do. Have faith and open up the story of your life to the world, so that they may know who lives in you because He who lives in you is greater than he who is in the world. When your life is over do not let your story be put on a shelf and collect dust but let your impact for the Kingdom of God be so great that long after you leave this Earth, your story will continue to grow in the lives of other for Jesus Christ.

Bradley Stubbs

People Follow the Latest Trend

The last major method I see used in the world today that lures people into accepting sin is the desire to follow the latest trend. I know this sweet little kid that my wife and I have been around for the majority of his life. He is just a little over two years old and an absolute joy to be around. As a baby, he was innocent, not knowing how to act or what to do. The only thing he thought he needed in life was his parents, food, and his bottle. As he became older, he started to pick up on things quickly. He started to understand some of the things on TV and what people were saying, especially when he began to talk.

He loves dinosaurs and can literally tell you more about them than I may ever be able to. He started to see commercials about some dinosaur figures, and then he begins to see them all over the stores. He even looked through a catalog and circled the ones he liked. Everything he saw in his world was screaming at him how amazing these figures were and how much kids loved them. He was convinced that these figures were the best thing in the world. What was interesting to me was that he recently began to say a new phrase. Every time he would see a dinosaur figure that he wanted on TV or in the store, he would say, "momma, I need that."

Even at his young age, the world had already tried to convince him that he needed the newest toy or trend it offered. This is a dangerous method the world uses because this method is used on us all throughout our childhood and follows us into adulthood. As a kid, we see these commercials and advertisements that tell us we need this new toy or gadget. We are convinced that we need this toy to be happy or that we cannot live without it. Many of us as a kid likely have also cried out in a store when passing a toy we thought we could not live without, "momma, I need that."

This is because the more the world can convince us that we "need" something it has to offer, the more we will chase after it while running away from the things we truly need. I mentioned that this method follows us into adulthood, and here is what I mean by that. As a teenager, the world convinces you that you need that car, that trendy outfit, or the newest smartphone. As a young adult, the world convinces you that you need a new house, a big TV for the living room with all the functions, and the newest gadget that will improve your life. After Gracie and I got married, we were flooded with advertisements in the mail telling us we needed to get all these things to make our life the best it can be. The advertisements are attractive, and they try to make us think that we were crazy for not having these items before. How on earth did we ever survive without them? People are drawn into this method and begin to follow whatever the world says we need, thinking they will be the happiest and most successful if they do so.

Looking back, it is really funny to see some of the trends that were widely popular when I was a teenager. Silicone bracelets were a big hit where I lived for a while. Every high schooler seemed to have one or more on their wrists. They had all kinds of designs, and almost every convenience store sold them. The crazy and more exclusive the band was, the better. I remember I had a giraffe colored one and a black and white one that I thought was the coolest thing. I wore them to school, and I felt like I was on cloud nine. After that trend ended, fidget spinners became the thing everyone needed. It started off with one type of fidget spinner and after about a month of this trend, there was so many different types it was unbelievable. There were even entire stores that opened up dedicated to selling them.

People jump all over trends. They trust the world to tell them what they need for their lives. They are convinced if they do not get the latest trend that somehow their lives are incomplete, or they will be left out. We believe that whatever is the most popular in the world must be good and something that we need. We have more trust and faith in the world to tell us what we need than God's Word. Sadly, people do not consider that even in world trends, the last four letters are e-n-d-s. All trends will come to an end. If I wore my giraffe-colored silicone bracelet out to the store today, no one would think I am the coolest person on the planet, and likely they would think the total opposite.

What can be equally as dangerous is when people follow the trends of who the world deems as popular and famous. The world will try and convince us that we need to be just like this a certain person or a group if people. I will give you a good example of how this works. When radio first came out, there was no hip hop or rap music; culturally, that was not something that interested people. As the culture changed, hip hop became very popular and people in our world wanted to be just like those stars by the way they danced, dressed, and acted. The world begins to look up to these people as leaders and role models in society. I know as a kid, my wife loved Taylor Swift. She thought she was the coolest person on earth. No matter what song she put out, she instantly loved it. Many kids are the same way with popular singers today. They anticipate their newest song to drop, and they want to talk, dress like, and support the same things they support.

People do not value going to church or being in community with other believers as they used to. I talked about earlier how busy Americans are today. Sports, activities, clubs, and social events have consumed our time. I know I loved playing sports when I was a teenager and young adult. Once I got very involved and serious about taking my game to the next level, I would have practice at least five days a week, and during the summer, I went to camps every other week.

Practice would go late into the night, so I stopped attending Wednesday night services at church. Camps would be on Saturdays and sometimes Sundays, so I would miss any youth summer camp and possibly even church on Sunday mornings. My main mentors in my life, besides my parents, transitioned from my student pastor and pastor to my coach and those athletes I looked up to at the next level. If our coaches told us to do something that maybe did not seem right or if they cursed on the field, that was just how things were now, times had changed, and we should accept that; these were our role models. If the coaches did not want you to go to church some days so you could practice more, then that was just how things were; again times had changed, and these men were our leaders.

This was the mindset a lot of my teammates, and even myself started to develop. The same is true with other activities, clubs, and social events. We spend so much more time in the things of the world than in the church that we start looking at the leaders of those things in the world as our main mentors. This has led to a transition from pastors and church leaders being the main mentors of people to the world's leaders being the main mentors of the majority of people. We follow whatever trend these worldly leaders say we should.

The truth is that people did and still do use music and other avenues to speak messages into society and because people love the music, show, movie, or etc. they many times pick up on the messages within these outlets and live those out whether good or bad. In the last decade or two pop and rap music have become very popular types of music, especially within the younger generation. There is nothing wrong with these two types of music by themselves, but many of the leaders in these types of music have put out messages that are getting more and more provocative. As I talked about earlier, a lot of popular music today talks about degrading women, smoking weed, getting drunk, cursing, and having sex. The lyrics are catchy, and the beats are really good, so people enjoy the songs, and they look up to popular artists as role models for how to live.

This is the current trend in our world today and the world makes it seem as if we do not jump on board this trend, that we are somehow behind the times or stuck in the past. I would argue and say that the world is the one that is stuck in the past. For centuries people have valued the things the world thinks more than what God says we should feel, think, believe, or do and jumped onto the latest trend, thinking it would bring them happiness and fulfillment. It is not hard to look back and see that time after time; this has failed us. People never end up finding true joy and are always searching for more, yet as humans, we are stubborn. We continue to follow the pattern of the world, thinking that this time things will be different, or this latest item or trend will actually bring us lasting happiness and make our lives better.

Today, young teenagers start singing along to these trending songs, likely not even realizing what they are saying at first. After they understand the messages in the songs, they are already hooked on them and still sing them because the world has convinced them that this is the direction people need to start going in, and this type of music is the best route for our world. They are convinced by supporting this they will find acceptance in the world and that will lead to them to finding love and peace themselves. Without knowing it, they have become victim to this method of the world.

I have talked to many teenagers that when they talk, provocative things come from their mouths. When approached about it, they said, well, that is how people speak today, or that is just how things are now; you would not understand. The world has convinced them that no matter what the songs, shows, and movies are promoting these days if the world now accepts it, then we should follow suit. If our leaders and role models now advocate for certain causes, then we should also accept those and advocate for them as well because that is just how things are today and the best thing for us to do is to follow suit. The truth, however, is that no matter what the world does on the outside, it should not change who we are on the inside. Cultures and customs will come and go, but morals and faith are here to stay. Unfortunately, many people today, even those that claim to be Christians, are like chaff that is blown by the wind. Whenever the next trend comes, they jump on it and let it take them wherever it wants. A lot of us are not firmly planted in God's Word as we are called. Look at what Psalms tells us.

"The wicked are not so but are like chaff that the wind drives away. Therefore, the wicked will not stand in the judgment, nor sinners in the congregation of the righteous; for the Lord knows the way of the righteous, but the way of the wicked will perish."

(Psalm 1:4-6, ESV)

Our lives should be so firmly planted in God's Word that when the wind comes roaring in (the newest trend comes out), we will not be carried away by it, but understand that just like the wind, worldly trends will come quickly and leave quickly, but God is the same yesterday as He is today and will be in the future. His Word is eternal, and He is the only one that will give lasting joy. If we jump on every latest trend, by the time the wind dies down we will end up somewhere we never wanted to be and our relationship with God will have gained quite a bit of distance. When we are firmly rooted in God, however, we will produce lasting fruit in our lives and prosper in all we do.

"Blessed is the man who walks not in the counsel of the wicked, nor stands in the way of sinners, nor sits in the seat of scoffers; but his delight is in the law of the Lord, and on his law, he meditates day and night. He is like a tree planted by streams of water that yields its fruit in its season, and its leaf does not wither. In all that he does, he prospers."

(Psalm 1:1-3, ESV)

How to Renew Our Minds

One of the best ways to not fall victim to this method if the world is to be cautious of any change that is widely accepted by the world. Most times when good change needs to happen, it is not very welcomed. Let me give you a few examples. Think about slavery in America. This was terrible thing, but a good portion of the population did not want to see it changed. Why? People wanted what they wanted whether it was right or not, and having slaves helped certain wealthy people make more money along with other things. Abraham Lincoln stood against slavery and eventually led America through the Civil War. He ended up abolishing slavery in America, but although this change was a wonderful thing, it was still not received well by many. He was later assassinated by a man that did not support this change. Martin Luther King, Jr. as mentioned earlier continued the cause of promoting equal right to people of color that live in the United States. He was also not welcomed by many in the world as during many of the marches he led, people were hit with batons, fire hoses were sprayed on people, and many were imprisoned. Later, Martin Luther King, Jr. would also face the same fate as Abraham Lincoln as he too was assassinated.

The greatest example of a wonderful change that was not widely accepted by the world was Jesus Christ. He came into this world to save the world from their sins. He lived a perfect life. He loved all people. He healed people, comforted them, helped them when they were weak, and even fed thousands of people. His cause was simple. All people had to do was leave behind their sinful lifestyles and follow Him. He would give them eternal life, forgiveness of sins, a peace that surpasses all understanding, and unconditional love. This was no trend, but a wonderful change that would be eternal. Instead of people jumping all over this, they spat in His face, cursed Him, beat Him, and nailed Him on a cross with a crown of thorns in His head, and left Him to die. Although this change was wonderful, people in the world wanted what they wanted, and they refused to give up the power they had in the world, their wealth, and their fame to follow the King of Kings.

The world is inherently evil ever since the Fall. So, when the world promotes change and it is widely accepted by the media and people in the world, be very cautious. Most of the world does not follow Jesus and most of the changes the world will make and promote will be from what the world feels is best or from what the world desires. Most of these things will not be God-honoring and we should be careful not to accept them until evaluating them in light of God's Word. When a wonderful change happens, it will likely be met with most hostility from the world because it will more than likely involve people abandoning their sinful practices to promote and live by the truth. It sounds like people would run to changes like that, but people are selfish, and the devil rules the earth for now, so when these kinds of changes start getting promoted, be prepared for the world to do everything it can to stomp them out. This, however, should not waiver you from standing up for the kind of changes God calls us to because although the world is against us, His love and mercy reign forever and following Him leads to eternal life.

"But you, beloved, building yourselves up in your most holy faith and praying in the Holy Spirit, keep yourselves in the love of God, waiting for the mercy of our Lord Jesus Christ that leads to eternal life" (Jude 20-21, ESV)

Just because the world changes in a bad way does not mean you have to. Sure, we should adapt to the changing culture around us so we can minister to people, but we should never waiver on our belief in Jesus Christ. That is the one thing that no matter what changes around us should stay the same within us. The devil rules the Earth for now, and the changes he supports are the changes the majority of the world will likely support. This should not discourage you, however, because one day Jesus is coming back, and He will establish His kingdom on Earth, and if you stand up for what you know He would want you to stand up for now and refuse to accept the things and trends the world promotes, you will be rewarded for it later. That reward will be far more precious than any reward or praise the world we will give for accepting what they tell you to.

"He will render to each one according to his works: to those who by patience in well-doing seek for glory and honor and immortality, he will give eternal life; but for those who are self-seeking and do not obey the truth, but obey unrighteousness, there will be wrath and fury."

(Romans 2:6-8, ESV)

"Then I saw a new heaven and a new earth, for the first heaven and the first earth had passed away, and the sea was no more. And I saw the holy city, new Jerusalem, coming down out of heaven from God, prepared as a bride adorned for her husband. And I heard a loud voice from the throne saying, "Behold, the dwelling place of God is with man. He will dwell with them, and they will be his people, and God himself will be with them as their God. He will wipe away every tear from their eyes, and death shall be no more, neither shall there be mourning, nor crying, nor pain anymore, for the former things have passed away."

(Revelation 21:1-4, ESV)

One way to avoid being swept up by the trends of the world is to learn how to be content in all circumstances. This is very challenging when we live in a world that tells us we should always be looking for bigger and better. I know for myself I sometimes get caught up thinking the grass will be greener on the other side. When I was at college, I wanted to rush through my last year to get out into the real world and start making a difference. Once I got my first job, I wanted to do the best I could so I could quickly move on to a bigger and better one. The issue is that sometimes bigger is not always better, and more importantly, it may not be where God wants you to be right now. If God has you where you are now, it is for a reason.

If we are always looking at what the next best thing is, we will miss our purpose and reason for being where we are today. Sure, where you are living may not be the nicest place or your job may not be the most glamourous, but while you are there, you should give it your all. Do not give it your all just to get something better, but because where you are is where God has called you to be for this season and because you desire to make a difference where you are. If God keeps you at that job for a month or three years, take every opportunity to pour into the organization and the people and shine a light for Him. When you leave, make sure the place you are leaving is better because of the impact you made upon each and every person you came in contact with.

For example, I know a lot of youth pastors that take a job at a small church simply to just get some experience on their resume' so they can eventually get that offer to go to a bigger church. This mindset is not from God but from the world and is the same mindset that leads us to accept the newest and latest trends. Our hearts are in the wrong place. These youth pastors should instead be grateful for the opportunity to pour into students each week. Often times, smaller churches have a very hard time trying to find quality leaders. So, if God has called you to lead a group at a smaller church, then be the absolute best leader, you can be for them. I currently serve at a smaller church, and I love it. For a while, I thought the bigger church, the better, but God really convicted me. Where He has put me has a great need for a strong leader. Many students I have encountered came from broken homes, were hurting, and in need of strong spiritual guidance. What an opportunity to make a difference! At a larger church that has had a solid student program for years, those kids may not need as much guidance, they have been blessed to have had good leaders their whole lives, but at these smaller churches, these students are spiritually starving.

Just like with a student pastor job at a smaller church, or someone working a less than glamourous secular job, sometimes God may call you to a bigger church or bigger company. There is absolutely nothing wrong with that, as you may be the right person at the right time to take that bigger church to the next level or to help change that larger company for the better. The problem arises when you have the mindset that bigger is always better and when you are constantly searching for the better opportunity. When we have this mindset, the devil will attack us hard and can easily begin to drive us into the pattern of this world and away from where God is truly calling us. If we can learn to be content wherever God has placed us and serve Him there with all our hearts, then whether He calls us to a bigger place or not, we will be blessed in all we do. Read the words of Paul below and reflect upon where your own heart is at.

"Not that I am speaking of being in need, for I have learned in whatever situation I am to be content. I know how to be brought low, and I know how to abound. In any and every circumstance, I have learned the secret of facing plenty and hunger, abundance and need. I can do all things through him who strengthens me." (Philippines 4:11-13, ESV)

Sometimes change in the world is not a bad thing if we are sure to keep our morals. Many times, we may have to change the way we do things to reach those that are lost. One way, Gracie and I have taught others to be in the world, but not of the world is by giving our students an alternative to what the world has to offer. We wanted to show them we do not have to totally abandon whatever the world promotes, but instead, we can choose to be in the world but follow the truth. A good portion of my students enjoy rap music right now. Rap and hip-hop music, as I mentioned earlier, seems to be the current trend. Most of the artists they listen to do no produce God-honoring music. So, we took them to a Christian concert with rap artists, pop artists, and a hard rock group that played the same type of music, but they had lyrics that were of love, hope, and worship to God. I encouraged them to invite their friends to this event. We had a good turn-out with many students that do not come often and one that had never been. During the concert, we danced like crazy, laughed a lot, and truly had a wonderful time. Many of these students had never seen that type of music performed by Christian artists. They were amazed and intrigued. After the message, that night, the student that had never come before ended up accepting Jesus as her LORD and savior.

That student immediately got plugged into our youth group. She ended up being a major part of helping us start our own student band. She even designed the logo that we still use for our band today. She became a leader in the youth group and a lead singer in the band. She later invited her sister to come to the youth group as well. After a few weeks, her sister started coming more than once a week and quickly became one of our most involved students. God continues to both of them in powerful ways for His kingdom. All of this started by just showing her another alternative to what the world had to offer. We still listened to the trending style of music; we just left out the provocative things the world accepts and promotes and replaced those things with things that are God-honoring.

This method is biblical as Paul was prepared to do whatever He could to share the Gospel with those that were different than him. He knew in order for him to reach the world, he had to reach people where they were at. Our world today is obsessed with following trends. A great way to reach the world around us is to take those things the world is obsessed with and turn them into something God would be proud of. Show them Who they should be obsessed with instead, while also showing them they can still do some of the things they love. Look at what Paul says in the first letter to the church in Corinth.

"For though I am free from all, I have made myself a servant to all, that I might win more of them. To the Jews I became as a Jew, in order to win Jews. To those under the law I became as one under the law (though not being myself under the law) that I might win those under the law. To those outside the law I became as one outside the law (not being outside the law of God but under the law of Christ) that I might win those outside the law. To the weak I became weak, that I might win the weak. I have become all things to all people, that by all means I might save some. I do it all for the sake of the gospel, that I may share with them in its blessings."

(1 Corinthians 9:19-23, ESV)

I remember when I served at a major summer camp and the impact that camp had on the lives of the students that came to it. We would see teenagers come in every week that did not want to be there. The only reason they came was because their parents made them, or a friend invited them. They would get off the bus with their earphones in, not wanting to hear anything anyone had to say. They would stand back from the crowd at first not willing to participate in the events.

The very first night of camp, we had what we called a Christian welcome to camp concert. We danced like crazy, had glow in the dark foam sticks, and jammed out to some Christian hip-hop and rap music at high levels. There would be beach balls flying and lights going crazy. You can imagine the shock on these students faces as they entered in the auditorium. This was not what they envisioned when they thought of a church camp or Christians in general. This was, well something they actually enjoyed. We begin to see them dance around, smile, and laugh.

Later in the week, we had beach volleyball tournaments, lots of recreational games, night activities, and we concluded the week with a really competitive relay race between all the groups that were there. Throughout the week, between all these fun activities, we had morning quiet times, Bible study groups, a message each evening along with worship, and church group devotions. We showed these students who Jesus was, what He did for them, and why a life dedicated to following Him was much better than a life consumed by the world. We begin to see these students that were shut off to the Gospel begin to be more and more involved and interested as the week went on. Many of these students, by the end of the week, accepted Jesus as their LORD and savior and opened up to us about struggles they were facing in their lives and asked for advice.

What is important to notice is that these students were consumed by what the world said was acceptable and they thought that Christianity was outdated and completely opposite. We simply showed them that just because culture changes, our beliefs should not. We could have more fun as a Christian, still doing many things the culture promotes, without doing anything provocative. Many of these students said this was the best week of their lives. We simply changed the way we ministered to fit the culture without practicing or promoting any of the sinful things of the world. This showed the students that they do not have to accept things in the world because that is what is trending, but they can choose to stand up for what is truly right while still doing many of the same things the world. They realized a life dedicated to Jesus was actually filled with much more joy than a life consumed by the world, and they felt a peace they had never received from living how the world told them to.

A Living Sacrifice

Throughout this book we have examined several methods the world uses to get us to conform to the pattern of accepting sin and denying the truth. After examining each method, we have gone over ways on how we can renew our minds back to God, and also ways we can help lead others away from the world and toward Jesus. Now that we know all this, the last thing I want to cover is the final question of what does it mean to be a living sacrifice? If we are going to sum everything up, how do we really become living sacrifices for Jesus?

Being a living sacrifice can simply be put to sacrifice the things you were living for and to start living for the things Jesus died for. It means we sacrifice our reputation in society to gain a higher reputation with the Father. It means we sacrifice our comfort and safety so others hurting can find hope and peace in Him. It means we sacrifice our desires and our will so we can live out the desires and will of the Father. It simply means we are willing to sacrifice anything and everything in our life for the sake of the Gospel because we love Jesus that much more than anyone or anything this world has to offer. We also know this is what we are called to that it would kill us not to.

I really love lemonade. To me it is one of the greatest drinks anyone could ever have. The best lemonade in my opinion is the one that is freshly squeezed and probably has some parts of the lemon floating around the glass. In order to make this delicious lemonade, it takes several lemons that are finely squeezed into the jar. See, no one would just take the lemon by itself and eat it peel and all. That would taste terrible. The only thing people love about lemons is what they have on the inside and what they produce when they are squeezed. The same is true in our relationship with Jesus. Jesus does not care about how you appear on the outside. If you tell your friends and family you are a Christian, you put it on your Facebook profile, or even if you go to some Christian events every now and then. Jesus cares about what is on the inside. What do you produce when the world squeezes you?

It is easy to be a Christian when you are not being made fun of for it or persecuted for it. When people attack you for being a Christian and the temptations and pressure of the world bear down on you, that is when the true test comes. The true you, the one on the inside that only you and God know, comes out, and the question begs, what person will the world squeeze out of you? Will the world squeeze out a true believer and one that will stand firm in God's Word despite what may happen to them, or will the world squeeze out someone just going through the motions, and when things are not easy, they will become like anyone else in the world? Only you and God know what person would be squeezed out today if the pressures of the world came bearing down on you. If that person is someone you are not proud of, then this is a wonderful chance to get your life in the right place with Jesus. Be a true living sacrifice for Him. Be the person that when the world comes bearing down, you produce everlasting fruit. You pour out love, joy, peace, patience, kindness, goodness, faithfulness, and self-control. Most importantly you shine bright in the world of darkness, unashamed of the Gospel of Jesus Christ. If the world squeezes that person out of you, just like Paul and so many others we have examined, the world will have to stop and take notice of the true, unconditional love of Jesus Christ found in you and realize that nothing else compares.

I think the biggest thing that holds people back from being a living sacrifice for Jesus is personal comfort, especially those that live in America. Why do you think so many people overseas are ready to do anything for Jesus even if they were to die? They are totally dependent on Him just like some were in the Bible. In America, most of us have been blessed with more than most people could ever imagine and we begin to value our things, jobs, social status, and wealth more than Jesus. We even begin to think we do not need Him and can-do life just fine on our own. We will be a Christian as long as it never gets messy. The truth is, when you become a follower of Jesus, things always get messy. The world will naturally come down on you because you are going to live contrary to the pattern the world wants everyone to accept. You scare those living in the pattern of the world and pose a threat of taking down all they stand for.

The thing is, if we are truly going to be followers of Jesus, we have to pick up our cross and follow Him. Jesus never once told us life would be easy or comfortable following Him but that you will live a life of purpose, and it will be worth it in the end. The disciples dropped everything to follow Jesus, and He used them to do incredible things for the kingdom of God. The question is what are you willing to give up in order to follow Jesus? Is there something or multiple things in your life that if Jesus told you to leave those behind and follow Him, could you do that?

"So therefore, any one of you who does not renounce all that he has cannot be my disciple." (Luke 14:33, ESV)

You may think to yourself that a loving God should never take you away from what you have worked for or for what you have gained. It is yours and you deserve it. The issue with that line of thinking is that nothing in this world including yourself is truly yours. You may think that it is, and people in the world will surely tell you that. The truth, however, is that without God, everything in this world including you would cease to exist. Without God everything we see including ourselves is absolutely pointless and void. See God is the one that gives life and meaning to all things including us, so this world is not ours it is His and He has allowed us to live and breathe in it. He has allowed you to have certain things and be successful in certain things, but if He desires for you to do something different or to give it all away it is because He has a divine plan for you. This plan will be far greater than anything you could ever imagine. You should be willing to follow His plan no matter what considering all that you have is His, and He is all knowing, you are not.

If you commit to following Jesus, you should expect Jesus to command you to give something away if it has become an idol in your life. The reason for this is because whatever you idolize in your life, everything else becomes a far second. Think about someone who is obsessed with their job. Sure, they love their family, friends, and church, but if it is two in the afternoon on a Saturday and work calls to inform them they need them to come into the office in an hour, where do you think they will be? They will not be at their kid's soccer game or on a dinner date that night with their spouse; they will be stuck at the office all night working their life away. See, work is not a bad thing, and we should strive to be the best we can be at work and put all we have into it while we are there just like everything else in life, but when we leave work, we leave work. This means we leave physically, mentally, and emotionally so we can be there physically, mentally, and emotionally for everyone else in our lives that are counting on us.

If you can never leave work at work or sports at the sport field or something else behind to do what Jesus is calling you to do, then that thing has become your idol.

That thing is what you will sacrifice anyone and anything else for including the calling God has put on your life. The thing or person you idolize can only be one thing in your life. So, if the idol in your life is not Jesus, then you will not sacrifice anything and everything to follow Him, but you will sacrifice Him if you have to for that idol you hold so dear. You will never be able to love the world and love God.

"No one can serve two masters, for either he will hate the one and love the other, or he will be devoted to the one and despise the other. You cannot serve God and money."

(Matthew 6:24, ESV)

Who or what is currently the master of your life? Who or what are you serving today? If either of those answers are not profoundly Jesus, then the next question you have to ask yourself is, how can I let go of that thing today? You have to find a way to let it go because if you never let that thing go that is holding you back from putting Jesus as the master of your life, then it will never let go of you. We can only serve one master in this life, and to be a living sacrifice for Jesus means that we are prepared to let go of anyone or anything our master tells us to in order to honor Him to the best of our ability. Jesus loved each and every one of us in a sacrificial way. The thing is, none of us deserve His love, yet He came to earth and died for all of us. He truly loves you sacrificially and unconditionally. If we want to please Jesus to the fullest, it means we have to love Him sacrificially and unconditionally, where no matter what, we will never let anything or anyone stand in the way of our relationship with Him and of what He is calling us to do. If you love Jesus in this way, you have become the living sacrifice He has called you to be.

"In the same way, let your light shine before others, so that they may see your good works and give glory to your Father who is in heaven."

(Matthew 5:16, ESV)

A good way to think about being a living sacrifice is to look into your heart and ask yourself, "If I were to die today, what would my testimony be?" If everyone that claimed to be a follower of Jesus loved Him sacrificially and unconditionally, then the world would look at Christians and see a strong group of people that are standing firm in one mind, one spirit, and striving side by side for the faith of the gospel. Our light would shine so bright into the world, and His love would radiate through us so evidently that the world would see the pattern they are living in will only lead to destruction, but the One that lives in us will lead to eternal life. If you want to change the world for Jesus, it starts with us right here and right now.

"Only let your manner of life be worthy of the gospel of Christ, so that whether I come and see you or am absent, I may hear of you that you are standing firm in one spirit, with one mind, striving side by side for the faith of the gospel, and not frightened in anything by your opponents. This is a clear sign to them of their destruction, but of your salvation, and that from God."

(Philippians 1:27-28, ESV)

CONCLUSION

I wanted to add this last section for anyone that has read this book, realized they have been living in the pattern in the world, and have a desire to give their life to the LORD. This a guide to help you make the greatest decision that you will ever make in your life.

How to Become a Christian and What Happens Next

1. **Admit that you have sinned. No one is perfect, and each one of us has made choices to do things in our life that God tells us not to.**

"For all have sinned and fallen short of the glory of God . . . If we say we have no sin, we deceive ourselves, and the truth is not in us." Romans 3:23, 1 John 1:8

Because God is perfect and without sin, our sin separates us from a relationship with the Creator

"God is light, and in him is no darkness at all." 1 John 1:5

"For the wages of sin is death . . ." Romans 6:23

Realize that no one will ever be "good" enough to get to Heaven by themselves because no one is perfect like God and we are all broken people.

"He saved us, not because of works done by us in righteousness, but according to his own mercy." Titus 3:5

2. **Believe that Jesus Christ is the only one who can save you from your sins.**

"And there is salvation in no one else, for there is no other name under heaven given among men by which we must be saved." Acts 4:12

Even though we have sinned, God loves us so much and still desires to be in relationship with us that He sent His only Son, Jesus Christ, to come down to earth, live a sinless life, and be the Savior for all who have faith in Him by dying on the cross for all our sins

"For Christ also suffered once for sins, the righteous for the unrighteous, that he might bring us to God." 1 Peter 3:18

Jesus not only died on the cross for our sins, but three days later, God raised Him to life again to prove that death was defeated. The penalty for all our sins was paid in full that day, and the opportunity to have a relationship with God and one day spend eternity with Him was made possible through what Jesus did for us.

"Christ died for our sins in accordance with the Scriptures . . . he was buried . . . he was raised on the third day in accordance with the Scripture" 1 Corinthians 15:3-4

". . . death no longer has dominion over him." Romans 6:9

3. Jesus tells us that all our sins will be forgiven if we have faith in Him, turn away from all our sins and commit to following Him for our lives.

"Everyone who believes in him receives forgiveness of sins through his name." Acts 10:43 "Whoever hears my word and believes him who sent me has eternal life. He does not come into judgment but has passed from death to life." John 5:24

"Repent therefore, and turn again, that your sins may be blotted out." Acts 3:19

"If we confess our sins, he is faithful and just to forgive us our sins and to cleanse us from all unrighteousness." 1 John 1:9

"If you confess with your mouth that Jesus is Lord and believe in your heart that God raised him from the dead, you will be saved." Romans 10:9

- Jesus never promises us that our lives now will be perfect or that we will never make a mistake again, but He promises us that no matter what happens in our life, His spirit will be there with us. He will give us love, joy, and a peace that surpasses all understanding in any situation that we are in if we look to Him and trust in Him. All He asks of us if that we make a commitment to do our best to follow Him each day, acknowledging that He is our Lord and Savior.

If you are ready to fully surrender your life to Jesus by asking Him to save you from your sins and be the Lord of your life, you can simply pray to Him something like this:

Jesus, I admit that I have sinned. I believe you are the Son of God and came to earth to take the punishment I deserved on the cross and saved me from my sins. I know you raised from the grave three days later and are alive today. I want to fully surrender my life to you. I turn now from my sins and ask You to forgive me. Please come into my life and be my Savior and Lord. In your name Lord, Jesus, amen.

What's Next?..............

If you have just invited Christ into your life, here are some things you can do to grow in your relationship with Him:

- Let someone know – If you have a church home, we encourage you to talk with someone in your church, but if you do not attend a church, please reach out to a Christian family member, or friend you know; I am sure they would love to celebrate with you.

- Get Baptized – This is a representation to the community around you that you have committed to following Jesus and you have been born again. The being immersed in water and then coming out represents you leaving your old life behind and starting your new life as a follower of Christ.

"Do you not know that all of us who have been baptized into Christ Jesus were baptized into his death? We were buried therefore with him by baptism into death, in order that, just as Christ was raised from the dead by the glory of the Father, we too might walk in newness of life"

– Romans 6:3-4

"Do you not know that all of us who have been baptized into Christ Jesus were baptized into his death? We were buried therefore with him by baptism into death, in order that, just as Christ was raised from the dead by the glory of the Father, we too might walk in newness of life"

– Colossians 2:12-13

- Get Plugged in – You are now a member of the body of Christ and God wants to use your gifts for His glory. We encourage you to get plugged into a local church and serve in some capacity. We all have different gifts, and we encourage you to use the gifts God has given you to serve Him through the Church. When the body of Christ comes together and we all use our gifts to serve Him, the body becomes stronger and can truly fulfill God's calling for the Church and the Great Commission.

"And Jesus came and said to them, "All authority in heaven and on earth has been given to me. Go therefore and make disciples of all nations, baptizing them in[a] the name of the Father and of the Son and of the Holy Spirit, teaching them to observe all that I have commanded you. And behold, I am with you always, to the end of the age."

– Matthew 28:18-20 – The Great Commission

"Now there are varieties of gifts, but the same Spirit; and there are varieties of service, but the same Lord; and there are varieties of activities, but it is the same God who empowers them all in everyone. To each is given the manifestation of the Spirit for the common good."

– 1 Corinthians 12:4-7

- Read the Bible to learn more about God and His plan for your life.

"Keep this Book of the Law always on your lips; meditate on it day and night, so that you may be careful to do everything written in it. Then you will be prosperous and successful." Joshua 1:8

- Be in prayer with God daily, sharing your joys, struggles, temptations, and to confess your sins.

"And pray in the Spirit on all occasions with all kinds of prayers and requests. With this in mind, be alert and always keep on praying for all the Lord's people." Ephesians 6:18

- Share your faith. You have just received a wonderful gift. Jesus tells us to share that gift with others. Make it a habit to seek out opportunities daily to share your faith with others.

"And Jesus came and said to them, "All authority in heaven and on earth has been given to me. Go therefore and make disciples of all nations, baptizing them in[a] the name of the Father and of the Son and of the Holy Spirit, teaching them to observe all that I have commanded you. And behold, I am with you always, to the end of the age.

– Matthew 28:18-20 – The Great Commission

We are so proud of your newfound faith in Jesus Christ. You are now a brother or sister in Christ. You have been adopted into God's family and have a place in Heaven for eternity. We wish you all the best in your new walk with Christ, and know we are praying for you every step of the way!

Bible Sources

- Crossway Bibles. (2007). *ESV: Study Bible: English standard version.* Wheaton, Ill: Crossway Bibles.

- *NIV Study Bible.* Zondervan Pub. House, 2011.

- *NKJV Study Bible.* (2018). Nashville, TN: Thomas Nelson.

www.ingramcontent.com/pod-product-compliance
Lightning Source LLC
Chambersburg PA
CBHW071450130726
47997CB00006B/2309